BEYOND THE FRAY

PARAMALGAMATION

BEYOND THE FRAY
Publishing

SHANNON LEGRO
G. MICHAEL HOPF

Printed in the United States of America

First Printing, 2020

ISBN 978-1-7344198-3-2

Beyond The Fray Publishing, a division of Beyond The Fray, LLC
San Diego, CA 92127

www.beyondthefraypublishing.com

DEDICATION

To our families

INTRODUCTION

para·mal·ga·ma·tion

> *noun*
>
> The action, process, or result of combining or uniting paranormal experiences which can, and should by all rights, be wholly separate. Truly inexplicable, nearly impossible to classify encounters with the strange, terrifying, and life changing.

When you hear the word *paranormal*, I'm sure you're like many who instantly think of lonely ghosts wandering the hallways of old homes, abandoned buildings or foggy graveyards with crumbling headstones. The reality is the word simply means something out of place, not normal, slightly off center, and almost always difficult to put your finger on. However, when we think of ghosts, we lump those all into a subcategory called hauntings, but what happens when someone has a run-in with a goblin or a wendigo? You see, there are many mysteries that fall under the definition of paranormal, but when you try to separate them out, it's hard if not impossible to do. It was this inability to do so that gave birth to the word *paramalgamation* and to this book. In fact, I named the 200th episode from my podcast, *iNTO THE FRAY*, this very thing because of the random para-goodness it contained.

As you turn from each chapter to the next, you'll read about encounters with things some of you have never heard of. However, they all have one thing in common: they're all strange, unexplained, which means, of course, that they're paranormal.

In the pages ahead, you'll be taken to an abandoned house that is the source of mysterious 911 calls. You'll hear from a woman who one night saw something that shouldn't exist, but there it was nevertheless in the glow of her headlights. You will read an account of something not human appearing while two friends sat down to innocently play with a Ouija board. These are a sampling of what you'll experience in the book. Some of these stories I've featured on my show, but others are new, never heard accounts told by the very people who experienced them.

The one thing I've learned in all my years of research with the paranormal is that those who've experienced the unexplainable are never the same after. Their lives have from that moment on taken a turn, some for the worse, while others, like me, use it as a springboard and become hooked. Their thirst to explain will be a lifelong endeavor, all done with the hope of one day finding a definitive answer.

I want to personally thank everyone who contributed their stories. I know it wasn't easy to come forward, so it's because of that I appreciate you even more. You risked ridicule and mockery to be here, and I hope telling your stories provides some comfort. And to my fans, again, thank you for always being there and listening, or now reading.

With all that out of the way, let me finish by saying that I sincerely hope you enjoy this collection of stories. So without further delay, sit back, relax, and go Beyond The Fray.

IT LOOKED RIGHT AT ME

There is an enduring question in the paranormal community, is the home haunted or are the people? So it begs the question, when a home is residence to more than its human occupants, who's to blame? Could a new family move in and experience nothing? Some of the details in Randy's story, from a covered-up doorway to an apparition acting like it's going through everyday life, may shed some light and give us an answer to that question.

***

In the early 1960s when I was about eight years old, my parents bought an older home in a suburb of Los Angeles, California. It was an older Spanish-style home, much like you see in Southern California, with tan stucco siding and a red clay tile roof.

My two brothers and I shared an exceptionally large bedroom. They slept in bunk beds on one side, while I slept in a single bed opposite them. At the front of the room, across from the door, was a large recessed area with an arched entry. This space was raised a bit higher than the rest of the room, making it look like a small stage. It was an odd area, we didn't use it for much, but there was always something about it that gave me a strange vibe, and no matter how bright our room was, this space was always dark, making it seem even more ominous. Needless to say, we avoided the area at all costs.

Late one night, I woke to a very strange and heavy feeling. I sat up but found myself immersed in almost complete darkness. I scanned my darkened room but couldn't see anything; then I heard a door. I looked with half-groggy eyes, expecting to see my mother or father in the glow of the light that now splashed into the room from the open doorway. There was someone there, and at first, I thought it was my father, as it appeared to be a male. The figure had one hand on the doorknob and one hand on the door frame as he leaned in and looked around. At the time, I chalked it up to feeling half awake, but the figure was completely black, as if it were absent of color or unable to reflect the light coming from behind him. I didn't know what to think, I kept assuming it was my father, but still something wasn't right.

The figure looked at me for a few seconds, leaned back out, and closed the door behind him. As I said, I thought it was my father just checking on us, but still, it seemed odd to me. With the door closed and the darkness swallowing me up again, I lay down, turned over to my side and settled in, facing the door to the room.

That was when it suddenly hit me, I was now facing my bedroom door, but that wasn't where I'd just seen the figure. Whatever or whoever that was had opened a door opposite the only door in the room. How was that even possible?

Instantly filled with fear, I screamed and bolted from my bed. I tore open my bedroom door and sprinted down the hall. I burst into their bedroom, woke them from a sound sleep, and began trying to tell them what I had just seen.

Wrapped in my mother's embrace, we followed my father back into my bedroom to find one of my brothers was awake, and the other still sleeping. Being my white knight, my father turned on the light, carefully looked around the room, but found nothing out of the ordinary. They put me and my brother back to bed, with implicit instructions to go back to sleep. My mother, being nurturing, sat on the edge of my bed until I finally fell back asleep.

Upon waking in the morning, my brother asked what had happened. In detail I described what I'd seen, his eyes wide with fascination as I got to the point about the thing looking at me. After I was finished, we timidly entered the dimly lit alcove to investigate. Upon our close examination of the space, we discovered something we'd never noticed in the past. There HAD been a door exactly where I had seen it open. Sometime over the years and no doubt before we'd moved in, it had been enclosed and plastered over. The doorway had once opened into the family room.

As disturbing as the incident was, it was only the first of two experiences I had in that house. Several weeks later, my father had to work an extremely late double shift. Unable to sleep while he worked late, my mother would stay up waiting. That night, she put my younger brothers to bed and allowed me to come out with her to watch a show on our old black-and-white television.

The room was dark save for the light of the television. My mother sat to my left, resting against a pillow on the arm of the couch, while

I sat wrapped in a blanket, my legs extended and my feet resting on a footstool.

To my left I saw movement. I snapped my head in the direction to see a small Pomeranian-type dog jump from my mother's lap, onto the couch between us, and then onto me. It ran down my blanket-covered legs and jumped onto the floor, disappearing instantly!

Startled, we both bolted upright, and in unison said, "Did you see that?"

I followed up and said, "Yes, a dog, right?"

She described the dog exactly as I'd seen it. She went on to tell me that she had just dozed off for a brief second and opened her eyes to find she was staring directly into the dog's face.

We were convinced we'd seen a dog, a real dog, so much that we checked the entire house, calling out with hopes it would show itself. When we couldn't find it, we went looking for how it could have gotten in and that maybe it went out the same way, but found nothing open.

It wasn't until later that I realized I'd never felt the dog nor its weight as it jumped onto the couch or ran across my legs.

We both explained what we'd experienced to my father, who only spent the next few days afterward laughing at us and teasing us about ghost dogs and shadow people.

Unexpectedly a month later, my parents sold the house only for us to move a few miles away. Not until years later, when I was fifteen, did my mother finally give me an explanation on why we'd sold the house and moved so quickly. She told me that she too had seen the dark man one night. With still a tinge of fear in her voice, she said she'd caught him watching her through the kitchen entryway as she was making dinner. So, filled with fear that she'd seen a person, she had called the police to report a prowler. I recalled that night the police came, but I never knew why they were there until then. I can still remember my mother keeping us kids out front while two police officers were in our house searching.

My father too had his own experience after we spotted the ghost dog. He apparently woke in the middle of the night to find a man standing at his bedside, leaning over with his face only inches from his. My father lashed out at the man, but suddenly he was no longer there. We moved out the next day. Later upon asking, my father simply described the man as nothing but a solid black figure.

I've never forgotten what I saw, nor can I not think about my parents' experiences, which resemble mine. I've come to think that the man I saw was nothing more than residual energy left over or imprinted on the house and that it repeats itself over and over in random fashion. I do wonder if one of the previous owners had the door sealed up and covered to stop the man from opening it; then again, it didn't stop it from doing what I saw. I don't believe that anything I've seen was interacting with me specifically, but then again, I can't explain it, nor do I have definitive proof of what it was doing. I only know what I and my parents saw was so profound that we packed up and moved.

I've been asked if I feel lucky or fortunate to have had my experience. I'd simply say that it's sort of a privilege to see a shadow man, but what still gets me excited was seeing the ghost dog. It looked so real, and except for not feeling it, I would still swear that it was there in the flesh.

I've not since seen anything, but when I hear someone bring up ghosts, apparitions, shadow people, etcetera, my ears perk, and my curiosity rises. It's nice to know I'm not alone and that others like me have had a run-in with the unexplained.

AN UNFOUNDED CALL

When someone with credibility like the deputy of a sheriff's department comes forward with an incredible and life-changing story, my ears perk up. In this case, a recurrent call to an abandoned home sets into motion a series of events that altered his thinking and even his career. This one has it all. Shadow people, missing time, Men in Black, and even a UFO.

***

It was 2009 and at that time I was a deputy sheriff in a rural county. I don't want to say which state, as I've already suffered the harsh consequences of what I'm about to share.

In the time frame of a month our dispatch had received three 911 calls from the same home. These calls were simply hang-ups; the second after dispatch would answer, the call would disconnect. What made these calls odd was they were coming from a house that was abandoned. Each time I'd take the call from dispatch and roll out to the property to find it empty, no furniture and no one around. I'd call back and declare it an unfounded call. This meant that you couldn't find anyone and that there was nothing to report. We chalked it up to issues with the telephone line.

Then the one night in question occurred, the night that forever changed my life. Over the radio I was notified that a 911 call had been placed from the abandoned house again. Like always, I headed directly there. I should note that I was working night shift, so when I was heading out to the property, it was dark out.

Like the other times before, I pulled up, got out with a flashlight in hand, and walked the perimeter of the house, to find no one nor any sign of anyone having been there. After my perimeter search, I headed for the house. I walked up to the back patio's glass sliding door and flashed my light inside. It was easy to see, as there weren't any blinds on the door, and just as I was panning to one side, I spotted what can only be described as a shadowy figure walking up the stairs towards the second floor. I was immediately shocked, as I was expecting the call would be unfounded like before, but I know what I saw.

I made a call in for radio silence; this is a safety precaution for whenever we go inside a house. I checked the door and found it open, so with my flashlight still in my hand, I opened the door and stepped inside. Before I headed to the stairs, I scoped things out to make sure there wasn't anyone else down on the main floor. Finding no one, I began my ascent up the stairs. As I was climbing, I took each step with care, as I wasn't sure whom I was about to encounter. Upon reaching the top, I searched the first room I came to and found it empty. I headed for the second, and this was where things began to get weird.

I stepped into the second room, and immediately my radio and flashlight stopped working. With no electronics and in the dark, I began tapping my flashlight against the palm of my hand, hoping it would turn on, but it didn't. A single window in the room brought in enough ambient light that I could see somewhat. I scanned the room, and in the far corner I saw a huge dark figure standing there.

Startled by seeing the figure and thinking at the time it was a person, I hollered out that I was a deputy with the sheriff's department. The thing didn't respond; it just stood there, not moving, as if it was staring at me.

I was very unsettled by this thing. The longer I looked at it, the more I realized it could not be a person. It was incredibly big and far too tall; I recall it being almost as tall as the ceiling. The best way to describe what I saw is to say it was the darkest thing I have ever seen; it was as if it were absent of all light, a void of some sort, but in the shape of a person.

I asked if they needed help, but still no reply.

Suddenly it moved towards me slowly and with a fluidity as if it was floating or hovering.

Spooked that it was coming at me, I hollered for it to stop, but it didn't adhere to my commands. Fear rose in me then; I reached for my weapon, then...

I found myself in my car. Yes, this is where it got weird and unexplainable.

I wasn't just in my patrol car, but I was driving down a desolate road about a half mile from the house where I had just been. I had no recollection of what had happened in the room or how I got to my car. I saw the time and it was later, almost an hour later. I had lost time and didn't have a recollection of what had transpired in between.

My radio crackled to life with people asking about me. I immediately hit my radio and said that I was Code Four, meaning I was okay. Not a few seconds after, I had an intense ringing in my ears, nothing like I've ever experienced in my life before. I then began to feel dizzy; it was alarming enough that I pulled my car over.

I wasn't panicked, yet I felt like something was wrong. Not wanting to make my condition widely known, I called my sergeant instead of broadcasting over the radio. I reached him with no problem and told him my situation. He instructed me to stay put and wait for assistance from other deputies.

The ringing in my ears subsided, yet my dizziness and vertigo were still present. Not wanting to pass out with my gun on me, I got out and put my duty belt and pistol in the trunk. With those now secure, I sat down on the side of the road, panicked, as I was having a hard time breathing. I removed my shirt with hopes it would improve my condition, yet it didn't. As I lay there, other deputies arrived. They promptly asked me what was wrong, but I could only tell them that I felt dizzy and short of breath.

An ambulance shortly arrived and took me to the hospital.

After endless questions and tests, with one doctor repeatedly asking me if I smoked weed, which I hadn't, I was released but with no diagnosis.

Back at home, I told my wife what had happened minus what I'd seen in the house, as I didn't want to scare her; plus I didn't know what I'd seen anyway. I got some sleep but was awoken just before six in the morning to knocking at my front door. Curious as to who would be there at that time of day, I opened the door to find two men dressed in black suits, wearing black sunglasses and fedora-style hats. This sounds so odd to say, but the best way to describe them was to call them the Men in Black, like from the movie.

Without prompting, they began to ask questions about what had happened the night before. I told them I'd gone to a house to respond to a 911 call, cleared the call, and drove off, only to call for help when I experienced dizziness. I didn't tell them about seeing anything at the house, as I knew it would sound crazy.

Upon finishing my story, they told me that I'd been released from my duties and that they needed my badge. I was shocked. I asked what I could have done wrong, and they replied that this wasn't disciplinary and that upon feeling better I could come back and reapply to work.

They handed me a release form and told me to sign it. Being that I was young and, to be quite honest, intimidated by these men, I signed the papers and gave them my badge and other things. They didn't say another word and immediately left.

I spent that day in a state of shock, as was my wife, who couldn't understand why they'd taken my badge. I didn't know what to do and couldn't for the life of me understand what I'd done to lose my badge and my job.

The following day I received a call from a buddy of mine who was a corporal in the sheriff's office. He told me that everyone was asking where I was and why I hadn't come into work. I told him that I had been released and that two men had come, broken the news, had me sign a release, then took my badge and other things. My buddy was now confused and said he didn't know what I was talking about, that no one at the office knew anything about me being released from duty. Word then came from my captain; like my buddy, he stated that no one at the office had released me. I explained I had the paperwork to prove what I was telling them. He ordered me to get it and come down to the station.

Not hesitating, I got off the phone and went to the dining table where I'd left the papers, but now they were gone. Panicked, I scoured the house but couldn't find them. I was freaking out; none of this made sense. I called the station back and told them I couldn't find the paperwork. This time though their tone had changed. They warned that they might press charges against me for theft of public property. Now I was beside myself. *How could they do this to me?* I thought.

Before getting off the phone, they gave me thirty minutes to find the paperwork and bring it down to the station. The second I hung up the phone, I again went back to tearing up my house, looking for the papers. Forty-five minutes went by and I hadn't found the papers. I was distraught, late to my office, and didn't know what this meant for my future.

The ring of the phone tore me away from my troubled thoughts. I picked it up to discover it was my buddy at the station. He said all was fine and that the county had called and said my badge was with them.

I was relieved. I asked again if all was good and if I was in trouble. He said no, I was good to go. He then told me the county had explained to the captain that I had had an epileptic seizure.

"Epileptic seizure?" I crowed in shock. I told him I wasn't epileptic, nor did I have a history of such things.

My buddy confirmed that was the reason and that I had for sure been released, but I wouldn't be charged with anything. That was the most I was ever told about that night or what the county had mentioned to my captain.

The phone call ended and so had my career as a deputy with that sheriff's department. I had been released from duty, but the rationale was a lie. To be honest, I was happy that I wasn't going to get into trouble, but still I had no explanation for any of it. Not the call, the shadow person, my dizziness, the Men in Black and so forth.

Months went by and I would still have some dizziness and the ringing in my ears. I went to the doctors, who then sent me to see several ear, nose and throat specialists. I was desperate to find out what was wrong with me. I even had MRIs done.

One MRI came back and showed I had a blockage in my left inner ear, but they couldn't tell what it was. They explained that this mystery blockage was what had to be causing my dizziness and ringing. I asked what could be done, and all they did was prescribe me some diuretics, which might help flush fluids out of my system, thinking that was what might be in my left inner ear. The medicine helped for a while, but later in 2009 the dizziness and ringing returned, with hearing loss in my left ear.

After a year had gone by, I decided I wanted to go back to work in law enforcement. Everywhere I applied, the process would go fine until it came time for the background and my time at the sheriff's department. I was told my old department wouldn't disclose why they released me, making it impossible for any new department to bring me on.

This is what's made this entire episode so odd and inexplicable. So let's break this down:

I go to a house that's been having numerous unfounded 911 calls; on my last drive by there, I have a run-in with what can only be described as a shadow person. I then find myself in my car driving, lost time, I get sick, I'm visited by two Men in Black, I lose my job, and now my old employer won't release to anyone why I don't work there anymore. I mean, this couldn't get any stranger. Still to this day I am struggling. I get sick every now and then, my ears still ring now and then, and I've suffered permanent hearing loss in my left ear. Years have gone by and still I can't get a straight answer on what happened during that time. I've personally contacted the sheriff's department, but they won't talk to me. All I want is an answer. Why did this happen to me? Was it a setup? Was it predetermined? Who were those men who showed up at my house early in the morning? How did they know about what had happened? How did the county get my badge? Why won't my old department talk to me? I've gone as far as hiring a human resources attorney, but because of the terms of my contract, I was on probation and at will. It's fine they won't hire me again, but why? Do they know something?

I don't know if I'll ever get the satisfaction of answers to all my questions, but what I do know is that moment in time and that brief encounter with that shadow person have altered my life for the worse. Not only has my health suffered, but strange things have continued to occur to me and my wife in the years since.

I've seen dark figures in my house and lurking around it. We find things moved or even thrown, and we've heard noises, more specifically we've heard what sounds like the cries of a baby coming from one of our bedrooms. I don't know if any of these things are related to what happened to me or the fact we moved into a new house and they're just coincidence. Again, I find myself at a loss to explain what's happened to me over the years. I can say that I do feel like I'm a bit cursed.

I'll wrap this up by giving a fair warning to all reading this: if you ever see a shadow person, don't confront it, don't be a hero, just run and don't look back.

THE MUTED PLACES

*W*hat would it be like to be suddenly muted, where no one around you could hear you when you spoke? Or even worse, not only muted, but suddenly invisible to those you were interacting with just moments before. In India, Ashe was the team leader for an important wildlife biology field expedition. He was by no means out there working alone, but quickly found himself feeling that way. Panic was likely not far off. Some may wonder if this is indeed what occurs in some cases of the Missing 411 by David Paulides. How close is the 'other side'?

***

I live in the beautiful country of India. The

country is vast and features not only busy cityscapes, but forests, both arid and high desert, and even wetlands. These areas are full of beautiful and often extremely dangerous wildlife; for instance, running into big cats in many of these regions is a real possibility.

I have always been fascinated by the natural world, so it made complete sense to make it a profession and work out of doors as a biologist amongst the amazing wildlife India is teeming with.

Most people in India are not very keen on discussing the paranormal, and the term *cryptid*, or a cryptid research group, for example, isn't something that really exists here. Ghosts, however, are quite popular. Many people enjoy passing down tales of haunted locations or encounters with a spirit, but if the paranormal is discussed, it's common for people here to tie it quickly to religion.

I have a couple of stories to share; the first one was relayed to me by a forest ranger I met while on a work project. We were out conducting a census on a certain breed of bird within a sanctuary in Rajasthan and planned on being out there for five days. This sanctuary was a wetland, not overly dense, and thankfully sans big cats. Our days comprised working during the daylight hours and congregating around the campfire at night. On the second night, many of my co-workers had wandered off, and I was about to join them when the ranger bluntly told me to be incredibly careful. I initially ignored this advice. While I might have been his junior, I had spent many years in and around the woods, so I knew my way around them and how to stay safe. He asked me to join him back at the campfire because he had a story to tell. I agreed and we went to the campfire to chat.

With a serious look on his face, he prefaced that the story took place about four to five years before in the same sanctuary.

He said he had been walking through the woods on a trail during daylight hours and saw something out of the corner of his eye. He turned his head to see a figure that seemed camouflaged with everything around it. How he was able to discern that something was there occurred because of the shimmer the thing gave off. All I could imagine is how the alien from the movie *Predator* would cloak himself.

He said the longer he looked at it, the more confused he became. He then detailed that a paralyzing dread washed over him.

This anomaly was around seven feet tall, standing on what resembled the tail of a snake rather than legs. Problem with that was the entire upper portion of it was human-shaped. It slowly dissolved from view, and he was released from his grip of paralyzing fear. He ran all the way back to the station but didn't initially talk to anyone about what he saw.

As an interesting side effect, he had a high fever and pain throughout his body for six days afterward. During his fevered sleep, he had many dreams, and this was where he began to put together what it might have been. His dreams were plagued with the Hindu God Shiva and countless snakes. The label he gave it was Naga. This can mean either a serpent or something tantamount to a mythical creature, half-human, half-serpent. He admitted to me, "This is something I should not have seen." This, of course, scared me a bit because I knew this man to be quite level-headed and very scientific-minded. Hearing this encounter on the second night of our expedition was interesting to say the least. Worth a mention...this trail happens to lead to one of the temples that sit within the sanctuary.

The next story I will share is my own, and it occurred in 2016. So, as mentioned before, I am a naturalist, and this puts me out of doors for my work. This fieldwork took me and my team to another wetland park, but really, it's more an 'urban forest' because it's not far at all from society. This sanctuary was about eight square miles in total, so not a massive tract of land. It is a protected area because of the many exotic birds that call it home. We were there specifically to census sand boas, as much of the water levels had been depleted over the years. It has one main body of water (at this time, it's nearly completely gone) that is surrounded by dense and sometimes spiny vegetation on all sides. The trees are not tall, but they are broad with a healthy canopy overhead.

There were twelve of us on the team, including a few volunteers...with me in charge. I was standing in a clearing, almost under a canopied area. I began to casually walk away from the others, entering the dry, tall grass. A few of my team were still behind me in the clearing, looking for boas. I continued to walk, maybe only forty to fifty paces from them, towards the watchtower that is on the property. It rises about twenty-five feet into the air—well above the tallest grasses. Two of my team were atop the watchtower, which was just to my left. It is important to note that the grass in this location does not even come up to my shoulders. I could see the man and woman on my team leaning forward on the railing of the watchtower, looking directly at me. At this point, I waved to them. They did not reciprocate the wave. I waved a few more times, with again no attention paid to me by the two. I made a quick mental note to tell them communication of any kind could be important out here, and that it was odd not to acknowledge me. I turned to go back the way I came.

I felt like I kept walking and walking but was not reaching the clearing where I entered. I have been in the field a long time and have not only an incredible sense of direction but can always easily retrace my own steps. I began to get worried and agitated now because I should have been only steps from where I began. I looked back to the two people on the tower and began waving once again. Once again, no response though they still seemed to be looking directly at me. I did not want to scream or yell because I was in charge, and who wants to be 'that' guy who gets lost! Since I could not find the clearing, I decided to head in the direction of the watchtower, because that I could see. It was, in fact, so close that if I had a twenty-foot-long stick, I could hit the two standing atop it on the heads. I felt nothing strange other than being lost and ignored by two of my team.

I could see the effects of my presence there. My shadow, my body moving the brush around me, and the grass breaking beneath my feet as I walked. The concern with my ego being bruised fell away, and I called the name of one of my team members. So many times, I lost track. Admittedly, at one point I was shouting. No response. Nothing. Now it was all beginning to feel extremely surreal and dreamlike. How could they not see or hear me? It was the afternoon, so it was, in fact, usually quiet as far as wildlife sounds go, but during this experience...it seemed unnaturally so. Several things added up very quickly to me, which compounded my confusion. First, there was even an airport not far, and you would hear a flight take off or land every few minutes. This had gone on for much longer than that, and I heard none of the reassuring airport sounds. Also...I realized the familiar buzz of the high-voltage power lines that ran through the park were not registering, nor did I hear birds or even the conversation of the two team members still perched in the watchtower. I did not exist to them.

Now I was freaking out. None of it made any rational sense, and my fear was building into anger. I started trying to calm myself and decided to try to head back to the clearing again, but this time I dived into even thicker brush than I entered. I had to try a different tactic. And incredibly, after only a noticeably short distance, I ended up in the exact same opening that I entered. The clearing. Other members of my team were there. They could see me, they heard me...all was suddenly very normal. I walked over to the main entrance for the watchtower and climbed it. I saw exactly where I had been and could give no explanation as to why I was so turned around or why the two people could not hear me. I really felt muted and completely invisible.

I have always had a love for the animals that inhabit the woods, and that is why I do the work I do. However, this experience has given me a truly deep appreciation now for the woods themselves. We know absolutely nothing about them at all. I'm not saying the woods are a sentient being, but they treat every person differently. I was profoundly disturbed for days after this, but I do still enjoy going into the woods. It has opened me up to many new avenues of possibilities in our world, but I can wholeheartedly say I do not want to enter a muted place ever again.

ZOO PLANET

*W*hat would you do if someone you not only knew well, but were even related to was returned after being missing for a time, but you swore it wasn't really them? What if you saw them being forcefully pulled into a dark void, a rip in time/space...for lack of a better term, by something likely from another realm altogether? What was done to your loved one while they were away? Would you ask them straight out about it...mention it to someone if they didn't? Mike had several very strange things happen in his life, but a missing cousin may top his list of odd occurrences.

***

I was about thirteen years old, which meant the year was 1993. It was July, and I was spending some of my summer at my grandparents' house in the rural countryside of New Jersey for the summer. What made it nice was the fact that many other family members lived close by, for instance my grandfather's sister lived next door, and a couple of cousins were just down the road.

Being a city slicker of sorts, I wasn't a fan of the woods, but when some friends and my cousins wanted to play hide-and-go-seek on a muggy and humid summer night, I went along, but I won't lie, I wasn't going to stray too far away from my fellow seekers.

Each of these properties were quite open until you reached the borders of them, and then it was thick brush and woods. My cousin and I were hiding in one of these bordering areas, and there was a decent amount of light coming from the houses we were nearest to, so we could see everything that was going on. We hadn't been hiding long when, unfortunately, our game was ended abruptly as one of my cousins (who was looking behind her while being chased) smacked right into one of the parked cars. She immediately began crying, and we all started emerging from our hiding spots to see what the ruckus was about.

My cousin Chris and I were paralleling a massive growth of tall rosebushes (these sported long, sharp thorns), trying to get back to the group and check on my other cousin, with me lagging behind about eight feet and trying to catch up. What happened next, I will never forget. For lack of a better term, a giant and very dark 'portal' seemed to open on the edge of the bush, and I could then make out the top portion of a torso. It came completely out of this dark, swirling space, and let me tell you...it was massive, semitransparent, and moved incredibly quickly. I could also make out what I assume was ears near the top of its head. The shadow reached out to my cousin, put a hand over his mouth and its other arm around his waist, and pulled him inside the portal. His legs never touched the ground after he was grabbed, and he never made a sound. This 'portal' immediately closed completely, with no indication it or the shadow being had ever been there. This entire incident spanned about three seconds. I jumped back, terrified out of my mind. I frantically proceeded to call his name and got as close to the rosebush as I felt safe doing.

Now my grandmother came out to call me inside. She hadn't heard me calling for Chris. I did plead with her to come out, and I proceeded to attempt to tell her what had occurred. Not only was Chris much older than most of us, about eighteen, but my aunt was not strict with him. So him being out later did not raise much alarm. Regardless of what I was telling her, she would hear none of it, only thinking that I wanted to stay out longer to play. She demanded I come inside, with even my grandfather coming out to give me a look to drop it. I then asked her if I could at least go next door and tell my cousin's family what I saw. She denied that request. So I reluctantly went in the house and to my room, tossing and turning, waiting for daylight so I could go back outside to look for Chris or any hint as to what had happened. As I lay there, I kept waiting to hear police sirens or the wail of an ambulance...but it never came, and I eventually fell asleep.

The next morning, I ran outside without eating breakfast, straight to the bush where I had witnessed Chris disappear. I walked all around the area, but there was no trace. No clothing, no blood, nothing. I went to my aunt's house and walked in, immediately asking if anyone had seen Chris. She replied simply, "Sure, he's in the back." Moments later, Chris and his younger brother emerged from a back room. I proceeded to ask Chris directly about what had happened, what had pulled him in the bush, why didn't you try to fight, etc. He only looked back at me like I was crazy, not only saying nothing but seeming to act very flippant about what I was saying.

Now, being pulled into one of those rosebushes should have left him covered with telltale signs, yet he was completely devoid of any marks or scratches. They both turned and headed to the front door, with me behind them. After my younger cousin headed outside, Chris turned around, looked directly at me, and flashed a massive, knowing grin. This scared the life out of me, and my mind was now racing even faster than it was before.

A very unfortunate medical condition befell Chris, where he would have periods of time being wholly unable to walk and having to rely upon a wheelchair for mobility. He would endure these episodes (some of them lasting up to a year) only to have it resolve, and he was able to walk once again. The oddest thing is, his doctors have never been able to diagnose him, and as far as I know, it remains a medical mystery. Last I heard, he was deteriorating even more significantly than before. I myself have my suspicions as to the origins of his plight and feel that other things come in and out of our reality whenever they like. I call this a zoo planet.

All these years, I've tried to convince myself it didn't happen...to push it to the furthest reaches of my subconscious. I have kept in contact with some of my extended family, but to be honest, I have not spoken to Chris again, and I don't want to...he scares me, because I truly believe the person who came back was not my cousin. I'll just conclude by saying that my initial opinion of the woods being an unpleasant place was heavily reinforced that night.

ROBERT

This episode is one of those that topped the list for not only post-air correspondence but claims of hearing EVPs within. Not to sway your opinion of what 'Robert' may have been, but the word vampire *is one of those some claim to hear within the recording. Spring break in Florida shouldn't be the time to worry about a party-crasher joining your group's little vacation, and usually it may not matter much...but Robert's unique mannerisms and peculiar abilities made it nearly impossible for a few of them to ignore.*

***

It was spring break, and like many others our age, we were in Florida to enjoy ourselves, which of course meant partying. A group of my friends and I made the journey from Indiana to Panama City, Florida, with dreams of staying on the beach, but the fact was we were low on funds. Not having a lot of money to spend on a hotel, we found one we could afford, and it wasn't good. First, it was miles inland from the beach and, second, in a bad part of town.

On our first night, we got an unexpected knock at the door. We opened it up to find a guy about our age. With a smile, he said his name was Robert and asked if we wanted to hang out and party. Right away I sensed something about him, I don't know how to describe it, but he had an aura, like he knew something we didn't. I know that may not make sense, but I just knew in my gut there was something off about him. I quickly dismissed it and, along with everyone else, agreed to hang out with him, because why not, it was spring break and, well, we were all there to party.

Later, we're playing cards, laughing and drinking. Robert, who was about two feet from me, shot me a look. I returned his gaze, and right then in the span of about five seconds, his face changed, like everything about it—his bone structure shifted; his hairline receded, grew shorter and changed color from a lighter tone to a darker one; his eyes also became darker. I was shocked to say the least. I didn't know what to think. My mind was trying to process what I'd just seen. I wanted to deny it, but I had seen it, no matter what I kept telling myself, I knew what I had just witnessed. It was surreal and unsettling. I know it sounds crazy, but right there in front of my eyes, Robert's face literally changed; he wasn't the same person I'd met hours before. A smirk stretched across his face, as if to tell me he knew what he had done and how it had affected me.

Not wanting to seem scared, I decided to act like I hadn't seen anything, got up and walked into the bathroom to get my composure. After a few minutes I exited but still felt uneasy, so I walked outside to get some fresh air and think about it. I still wanted to deny I'd seen what I'd seen, but each time I'd dismiss my denial. I had seen Robert change his face, and I knew just then I'd never unsee it. Not wanting to seem too startled or call attention to myself, I went back in the room and sat down. I saw his gaze on me, but I ignored him. I did wonder at the time if my friends had noticed, but no one said anything. The rest of the night went on without anything strange or odd, but I was still trying to come to grips with what I'd seen.

The next day we made it to the beach. As I sat watching the waves come in, one of the girls who had come with us from Indiana came up and sat next to me. She looked at me and said, "Robert said he made his face change for you too." I didn't know what to think or say, so I got up and walked off.

Besides the shock of his face altering, his presence alone made me feel uncomfortable enough that I risked going through his things after he fell asleep one day. He didn't have a bag, nor did he carry a wallet, which meant I didn't find an ID or anything that confirmed who he was. The only thing he did carry was a notebook. Curious, I looked through it, hoping to find out if he was who he said he was or I'd find some clues about him. What added to his strangeness was the fact that the only thing in the notebook were names, nothing else. Pages and pages of names, hundreds to be exact. That was very odd.

Something else I noticed about him that struck me as odd was his clothes, which consisted of what he wore; he had nothing else. The clothes themselves didn't have labels or brands. I don't why I thought that was strange, but when I looked at his stuff that one night, it stood out to me.

Another observation I had of Robert was just how smart and well-mannered he seemed. He was very articulate, and his vocabulary and worldliness weren't in alignment with his age. I couldn't shake it, but he seemed older, much older. Every time he spoke, he just had a way with words and seemed to know things that someone his age wouldn't know. Also how polite he was struck me, as someone who was acting much older, or at the minimum someone nineteen or twenty wouldn't talk with such politeness to their peers; it just seemed odd. And before I forget, I never remember him eating or drinking. I've searched my mind for that memory, but I can't recall; isn't that weird? Who doesn't eat or drink?

The end of the week eventually came, and we drove back to Indiana. After all these years I still can't get Robert out of my mind. However, this will seem weird to say, I don't remember what he looked like. I have an image of what I think he looked like, but I can't quite recall his face. I know his face changed, as I vividly recall reacting to the incident, but I'm unable to recall what he looked like.

My inability to get past that time caused me to reach out years later to my friends who were on the trip with me. My one guy friend said he remembered Robert but couldn't recall anything else except the fact that he was odd. I then contacted the girl, and she was taken aback by my reaching out at first. In our conversation she said that Robert changed his face several times. She also mentioned that he'd say odd things to her, like he said something that still to this day she hasn't forgotten. He said, "I can't believe you've not met someone just like me before." To give context, he said that after he had changed his face for her. I can only assume there are more beings like Robert out there.

Something else she told me gave me pause, and that was that he could not only read her mind but also speak to her telepathically. This freaked her out, yet she never told anyone. She also disclosed that she and the other girl on the trip were attracted to him, not in a sexual way but more deeply intrigued. Like them, we all seemed to hang on his every word.

It's been a long time, but I can say that I haven't come to any conclusions about what Robert was and what I saw. It has helped talking with my old friend about it, but if I were asked today if I thought Robert was still around, I'd say yes, but I'd add that he's probably still the same age. I say that because I can feel it deep in my bones. I just know he's out there and still the young guy I met all those years back.

With that said, what does that make him? Was he a normal person? No. Was he an angel or a demon like my one friend said? I don't think so. Or was he a vampire? Who knows, but even Robert mentioned vampires when he was with us. It was such a peculiar thing to bring up that my friend mentioned it to me when I contacted him recently. So was Robert a vampire with the ability to shape-shift and read minds? Who knows? Was he a fae? Someone has asked that too. Again, I'll never know, but I know one thing for sure, he was not your average run-of-the-mill nineteen- or twenty-year-old kid; he was something much more. And I'll finish by saying that I do feel fortunate to have had the experience. I know it's not as thrilling as, say, coming face-to-face with a Bigfoot, but it was one I'll never forget, and it has confirmed for me that the world is a much bigger place than most people think it is.

THE BOULDERS

When Chris first told me his story on my show, I wasn't sure what exactly Chris had encountered. To be very honest, to this day, I still don't know what it was. Yes, I have my theories and I won't say them now for fear I'd spoil what you're about to read. But what I will tell you, and I say this with confidence, I would have been terrified.

***

I'll never forget the night I'm about to tell you for a couple of reasons. First, our family was having financial troubles, which of course puts a lot of stress on everyone, and because of what I encountered.

My father and I had gotten into a heated

discussion resulting in us just walking away from each other without resolving it. I went into my room, slammed the door, and began to pace, the thoughts and emotions of that fight still lingering like heavy weights. I don't know why I recalled it at that moment, but I did remember that I'd left my truck at my grandmother's house, who lived a few miles away. Still filled with anger, I got the idea that I needed a walk to cool off, and while I was going to be out, I might as well go get my truck.

Without uttering a word to my father about where I was going, I headed out. The second I closed the door, I found myself immersed in darkness save for the twinkling stars above. Eventually my eyes adjusted enough that I wasn't walking in pitch black, but it was near impossible to see anything at a distance.

As I made my way up the road, my thoughts were preoccupied with the fight and our family's financial problems. I wanted the best for us, but I couldn't help but be mad at him. To my right was a large boulder field associated with an old rock quarry that stretched a ways alongside the road. It was here that everything went proverbially south.

I heard a moan come from just above the boulder field. I found it odd, so I stopped. I thought it had to be a coyote or something. I was still hot under the collar and thought that if anything wanted to mess with me, I'd just bash it in the head with a rock or something. My thoughts now back on my family troubles, I began to walk again.

A second moan or call sounded, but this wasn't near where I heard the first one. I don't know why, but I thought it was a reply to the first vocalization. Right on the heels of the second call came a third, then a fourth and a fifth; all came from different places and all now behind me.

I listened as whatever was making the sounds converged on each other, it was as if they were calling out to the other, trying to get their bearings. The calls kept echoing from behind me until I could tell that they were now together. Within a second of grouping, they headed towards me from behind.

I continued to walk, but now I was fearful. *What is behind me, and why is it coming towards me?* I thought. I nervously looked back several times but couldn't see a thing though I knew they were there, as they kept making sounds. Closer and closer they got until, without notice, about thirty feet behind me, everything went silent, eerily silent. I strained to see, but it was impossible to make anything out.

I heard them advance, the distinct patter of feet or paws on the gravel road. Like a well-trained team working in a coordinated fashion, they spread out around me in a half circle only about twenty feet or so from me. Then a clicking sound began. It was another type of vocalization and reminded me of the Bushmen from the movie *The Gods Must Be Crazy*. One would make a clicking sound, then another a few seconds after the first paused.

This clicking repeated back and forth. I knew coyotes don't make clicking sounds, and couldn't quite understand what was there. I'm not sure why I thought it at the time, but the clicks back and forth sounded like they were talking to each other, like it was a form of communication.

The entire time this was going on, I walked at a good clip down the road. I constantly looked over my shoulder with hopes I could see something, but I didn't; this only added to my fear of what it could be. The clicking continued, making my fear rise, but then something else began to occur, something I never expected...I started to feel drowsy. Yeah, I know that sounds odd, as here I am being followed by something, yet I couldn't shake this intense feeling of fatigue. The boulder field was still to my right, and in the center, I could barely make out a large one, big enough that I could crawl onto. I headed directly for it. Looking back on that night, I think it looked like a safe place. It was clear of any sagebrush, so nothing could hide. I got onto the rock and sat down, thinking I had a vantage point of some sort, but more importantly if I rested for ten minutes, I could keep pressing forward to my grandmother's house.

As I sat listening and straining to see, I felt the weight of fatigue keep growing. The clicking had stopped, and I had not heard any other noise. Whatever had been following me, my mind still trying to convince myself that it was coyotes or something, had moved on. With a sense of reprieve and unable to literally hold myself up from the unusual crushing fatigue, I slumped onto my left side and fell asleep.

To this day I don't know how long I had been asleep, but I do know that I was awakened by something touching the back of my head. I sprang up to find it was still dark out and with wide eyes scanned around as best I could. Behind me I heard the patter of what sounded like bare feet racing away from me on the rock. I spun around with hopes I'd see something, but it was gone. Filled with fear again and with a burst of adrenaline, I jumped to my feet and headed off towards the road. I was now determined not to stop, I would make it to my truck, and only then, if I felt the need, would I sleep.

Not a minute after I began my march towards my grandmother's did the clicking start again. Just like before, the clicks bounced around, from my left to my right then behind me. I was confused, scared, and still had a distance to go. I thought about running, but the crushing fatigue again spread across my body. I didn't want to stop again, I was determined to keep moving, so as a last-ditch effort to fight off the drowsiness, I started to hit my chest hard, shake my head and belt out loud screams. All the while I was doing this, the clicks were still around me. I can't express just how confused I was. How on earth could I be tired? None of it made sense, and no matter what I did, I couldn't fight off the fatigue. It almost felt like someone had drugged me. I suppose that's the best way to describe it, like I had no control over my own body, and anything I did, I couldn't shake it.

The drowsiness became so intense that I could barely walk, my head slumped, and I almost fell numerous times. Each time I lifted my head, I tried to get my bearings, but soon I lost track of where I was. I was so disoriented I probably could have walked off and into the river or could have been headed in the wrong direction.

The fatigue had now reached a tipping point. I could barely lift my feet, which now only shuffled on the ground. I either clipped a rock or lost my balance, but I recall falling face forward onto the ground. My knees hit first; then I was able to catch my body with my hands. I shook off the fall but was unable to stand. All I could think was I needed to keep going, so doing all I could, I began to crawl, but after a few feet I couldn't even do that. I paused for second to grit myself for what I needed to do, and that was get back up. Using every ounce of energy, I managed to push my upper body up from the ground but was still on my knees. I scanned around for anything that could provide safety and sanctuary, but I could not see a thing. I was now beyond scared; I was beginning to become truly terrified.

Not yet ready to quit, I kept looking from left to right; then I spotted what looked like a massive boulder, its sandstone color making it light enough for me to make out. It appeared tall enough that I would have an advantage over being on the ground itself. Filled with hope, I used all the energy I had to get to my feet and stumbled towards the boulder.

I was out of it, my mind could only focus on moving each foot forward, and if there was something next to me, I wouldn't have known. Heck, I can't recall if the clicking was still going on, I was that confused.

I reached the boulder, the side that faced me was sloped, and under normal circumstances I should have been able to walk right up it. The slight slope might as well as have been like scaling Mount Everest. I dropped to my hands and knees again and slowly crawled my way up. I reached the top but realized that the boulder, no matter how tall, would not provide any sort of safety from whatever had been following me. It didn't matter though; I was done. I had spent all my energy just making it to and up the boulder. I diligently lowered my body down onto the cool stone and resigned myself to my fate. If there was something sinister out there and it wanted to get me, it would. With my fate sealed and unable to even keep my eyes open, I pressed them closed and passed out.

Like before, I awoke, but I was now flat on my back. I opened my eyes to see the tranquil star-filled night sky above me. A grunt sounded above where my head was, followed by a similar sound down where my feet were; then the sounds of movement came from my left. My fear was still present, but I still didn't have the strength to even move. As I closed my eyes again to pass out, I recall thinking that I was surrounded.

Again I awakened, but now I knew it'd been a while, as I could see the sun rising over the mountains. I shot straight up and scanned my surroundings, looking for anything or anyone. After finding I was alone, I immediately began to examine my body for wounds, even counting my fingers to make sure I had all ten. Upon determining I was safe and unharmed, I sat and thought about my experience. I didn't have an answer for any of it. I still to this day don't know who or what was around me, but something was there. I finally made it to my grandmother's house, got my truck, and went back home. I never did mention my story to anyone, as it sounded crazy.

Listen, I know it seems odd to be fleeing from something but your desire to rest is stronger. I get all of that, but all I can say is it happened, and I wish I knew why. I wish I had an answer for why I lay down and slept while something was following me. I'd also like to know what was there. I don't think it was a Bigfoot, because I've never read about them making clicking sounds or being able to induce someone to sleep. The closest thing I think it could have been was a small creature my great-grandmother called the Sheep Eaters. And lately I've wondered if I was glamoured by a group of fae. I can go on and on about what it could have been, but the thing is, I'll never really know, as I never saw what it was. What I do know for sure is I was not alone that dark night in that boulder field.

A LIFE HAUNTED

I often say how invasive it is when activity is present in your own home. And even worse, when it's in your bedroom on a nearly nightly basis. If you heard little feet pattering around belonging to something you couldn't see, or witnessed a shadow person looming over you, or a disembodied torso executing the act of breathing...could you continue to sleep there? Could you ever again get a good night's sleep anywhere? In this next chapter, you'll find even the act of moving didn't tamp down the amount of activity Jordy was plagued with.

***

My younger brother and I grew up in a toxic

and abusive environment. I did not realize just how bad it was until I met my girlfriend and the mother of my child. Upon learning of my childhood, she told me that my early life wasn't normal and that most parents aren't abusive. I suppose I sort of knew this in some ways, but still, as a child with no other influences, I just assumed that getting slapped, kicked, or screamed at by my father was just the way life was. Now before anyone assumes my mother did not participate, she did in her own way. However, like most things, they do come to an end, and my last day having to suffer under this was when I was sixteen. It started like it normally did and ended with me taking a stand. He backed away, and I stood there, a grin stretched across my face. I left the house and never returned; that was eleven years ago.

The reason I felt compelled to preface my paranormal encounters with my abusive childhood is because I think it might play a role with my sensitivity towards such things.

I've even read theories that abused children can be more open and have a heightened state of awareness.

Now that I've given you a glimpse of my childhood, let me begin with my first encounter. It happened when I was about nine, which meant my little brother was four. His room was on the first floor, next to the bathroom on the left-hand side of the hall. On the right was my parents' room. My bedroom was the attic; while I had my privacy, I also had to go all the way downstairs to use the bathroom. So on this particular night, I woke with the urge to use the bathroom. I went downstairs, and as I was walking past my brother's room, I saw a flickering light on his ceiling. I instantly thought this was weird, as it was so late. I stopped and peeked in to see him sitting in front of his small CRT TV. The screen was nothing but static, yet he was staring at it. What made the entire thing even more strange was he was whispering, like he was talking to the television. I thought for a second that something could be off, then brushed it off as my brother being weird, went to the bathroom then back to bed.

From here on things escalated. He told his teachers our father died, which was not the case. He vandalized school property, and when asked, he'd say, "They told me to do it." Who were they, and why were they telling him to do bad things? I didn't know what to think, but it was apparent my four-year-old brother was dealing with something sinister. As I think back, I can't recall my parents acting on it at this point except asking him why he was doing what he was doing.

I was concerned to the point that I knew he needed someone to watch over him. I took his mattress and pulled it up to the attic so I could keep an eye on him during the nights. This helped and we grew closer. During the three months he slept in the attic with me, I'd ask him to describe what he had seen and who 'them' were. What he said chilled me to the bone. He told me there were two 'light persons' and a lot of small 'dark shadowy people'. The dark people would try to hit him but couldn't hurt him, as their strikes phased through him. My father, he was of Indonesian descent, eventually had an 'auntie' come, and she performed a cleansing of the house and my brother. After that, all seemed to go back to normal. However, my own experiences were just about to begin.

It's hard to recall just when, but I believe I was fourteen. I had fallen into a state of depression and felt estranged from my family. I became what could only be described as a recluse, always holed up in my room only to come out to go to school or get something to eat. It was during this time that I had my first shadow person visitation.

I was sleeping on my back, and I remember waking up in the middle of the night. My entire body vibrated and shook. My eyes felt like a hot poker had been stuck in them, as they burned. I blinked numerous times to get the burning sensation to stop, only to then see a dark figure hovering over me. I was in shock, frozen in fear.

If there was one thing I was most deathly afraid of at that time, it was creepy bedroom visitors. The thought of something coming into your room and lingering while you are asleep is very disturbing, and back when I was a kid, the very thought of it terrified me. There is something very vulnerable about us while we're asleep; we're incapable of defending ourselves. It's just very unnerving. My phobia of lurking night visitors was born after watching *E.T.* when I was four years old. My father thought it was a good idea to fast-forward to the part where Elliot and E.T. met in the field at night and screamed their lungs out. Needless to say, I was terrified. He did rewind the movie to the start, and we watched it in full to show me the alien was nice, but it didn't work. It left me with nightmares and anxiety for many years.

Anyway, going back to my visitor, it appeared it was studying me, its head slightly moving as if to see me better. It drew closer and closer; my fear rose. I didn't know what to do. It eventually got so close all I could see was pure darkness; it was so dark and black as if it were completely void of any sort of light. I managed to blink, kept my eyes closed for a moment, and opened them to find the thing gone. I lay there for some time before I could finally go back to sleep.

Unsure of where the thing came from, I barricaded my door every night with stacks of books and other items, but that wasn't enough. I slept completely covered under my blanket in a fetal position facing the wall every night, only a small opening near my mouth so I could breathe. It didn't matter if it was summer, I preferred sweating profusely over the immense fear I had of looking into my room, afraid of what I might see. At this point I hadn't even read about gray aliens or paranormal stuff. To make things worse, my dad found out I was barricading my door, so he removed my door. Yep, he literally took the door off the hinges, leaving me with a large dark doorway to stare into. When he asked why I had done it, I lied and told him I was afraid of burglars.

To add insult to injury and no doubt complicate my life with added terror following the sighting of my first shadow person, I often heard the distinct sound of tiny feet pattering around my bed at night as if there were children running barefoot in my bedroom. It wasn't until many years later did I wonder if those footfalls were the small dark figures my brother had seen.

Fast-forward weeks later and chalk up another strange and scary sight. I woke suddenly, as something had set off the backyard light's motion sensor. Curious, I went to the window, and what I saw was shocking. There in the light stood a white naked humanoid, its arm hung over the fence as if it was ready to unlock the gate. As I peeked down at it from what I thought was the security of the blinds, it looked up at me with a devilish grin stretched across its pale face. This thing appeared to be genderless, but somehow, I knew it was a male. What made the thing more terrifying, as if seeing a naked humanoid-looking creature wasn't enough, was it knew I was there even though I was hidden behind the blinds. As soon as I laid eyes on it, it returned my gaze with that creepy smile and vanished in the blink of an eye. I often wonder to this day if I'd seen what many call a rake, but it wouldn't be the last time I would have an encounter with such a thing.

Of course, that didn't end the things I saw over my teen years, but I want to now jump ahead almost ten years to illustrate a point I want to make. I don't think my house was haunted as much as I am haunted. Yes, I wonder if I could be a catalyst or at least able to see things that are seemingly more prevalent than we think but are unable to see. I wonder if my years of abuse somehow opened my mind up, enabling me to see what is normally unseen. This now leads me to my next encounter when I was twenty-three. I had just bought a house with my then girlfriend.

I was asleep, of course, it seems the things like to come when I am the most vulnerable, and my side of the bed was next to the entrance of the walk-in closet. (Yeah, another door opening.) I woke up and like before was unable to move. Towering over me, its head almost hitting the ceiling, stood a dark shadowy figure. Like before when I was a teen, I was frozen with fear. I wanted to move but couldn't. Was this thing the cause for my inability to move, or was it my fear? I had no idea, nor until this day do I know for sure, but it doesn't matter. There I was again in the presence of this thing, and all I could do was stare at it with wide eyes. While this thing looked like the one from many years before, I felt it wasn't the same creature or entity. With my only defense being my ability to close my eyes, I did just that. I pressed them shut and opened them to find that whatever it was, was now gone.

More years passed, I broke up with my girlfriend at the time, sold that house, and I moved into another house, but this time I was a roommate with two other people. I had my own room but didn't have much else, as I couldn't afford it. My bed was on a makeshift frame of pallets, and I didn't have curtains, meaning I normally woke when the sun rose.

My current girlfriend and I had just started dating. One night as we slept, her head on my shoulder, I recall feeling pressure on my feet. Again, the vibrating sensation washed over me. The pressure on my feet increased; it was as if they were being pushed down, like something or someone was sitting or leaning on them. Suddenly, I felt something quickly crawling up my body. Fear rose in me followed by a cold shiver. Something else was in the room with us, and it was on me, but what was it? The best way to describe the crawling on my legs is to say it felt like small hands tapping or pressing against my legs in a march towards my face. My fear rose to a crescendo. I wanted to move but could not; I was frozen. I imagined the worst sorts of things and fought to move, my mind begged for my body to respond, but it didn't. Then as fast as the sensation had presented itself, my motor function rushed back, but at that exact time, the pressure on my legs disappeared.

My haunted life continued, and this next experience highlights what I mean about it was me who was haunted or at least sensitive to such things, not a particular place.

The year was 2015 and my girlfriend and I went on vacation to a Greek Island called Kefalonia. As it turned out, our first two days there landed on a national holiday, making it impossible to rent a car, meaning we had to walk everywhere. During our exploring of the island, we found a restaurant where we wanted to have dinner, which was thirty minutes from where we were staying. What we didn't take into account was the fact we'd be walking back in the pitch black of night.

After having a great meal, we began our long and dark walk back. Our route was along a narrow and winding road, and in order so we could be seen by oncoming cars, we had the lights from our phones on. As we happily marched along, we sang the tune from *Snow White and the Seven Dwarfs* and other fun songs to pass the time and to have fun in our situation.

What happened next, I'll never forget. As my girlfriend was feet in front of me, singing her heart out, I suddenly heard someone walking up behind me, but before I could turn to see who it could be, a distinct female voice hummed in my ear. I spun around and was instantly filled with a cold spine-tingling chill. I told my girlfriend what I'd just experienced. She didn't question me at all, as she knew about my past encounters. We rushed as fast as we could back to our hotel.

In 2016, the paranormal activity ramped up, and I can only assume it was a combination of my own senses and the new place we moved into. It was a first-floor apartment near the old city center. The building itself used to be an old house that had been divided into a series of very small apartments. To give you an idea of how small this place was, the dimensions of the apartment were forty-nine feet long and thirteen feet wide, so yeah, a little less than six hundred and fifty square feet. On one end we had the kitchen with a balcony and the bathroom, on the other end was the living room, which faced the street. The bedroom was in the middle, which could be closed off by sliding doors off the narrow hall, which connected the two opposite ends.

My first experience in this apartment happened about two months after we moved in. Like all the other times before, I had been asleep only to awaken with my body vibrating and paralyzed. Since I was familiar with sleep paralysis, I didn't freak out; on the contrary, I was mad. All I could think at the time was, "Not again!"

When I opened my eyes, I saw it, a towering shadow person next to my bedside; its body hovered over me as if it was staring at me. Like I said, I was mad and struggled to break free of my paralysis. I desperately wanted to scream or even move an inch. What's strange is the harder I fought, the more my body vibrated. I also noticed that each time I struggled to move or speak, the room got fuzzy. I didn't let the vibration or the fuzziness distract me, I kept fighting to move, and just like that, I snapped out of it, and just as my freedom of movement was restored, the figure disappeared.

This exact encounter happened three more times in about the same way, but it got more difficult to snap out of it. The harder I fought, the harder I started to vibrate, and the second I did, I'd simply fall asleep as if nothing had happened, so weird.

Another creepy encounter that deviated from the shadow person was waking to find a bluish gray emaciated rib cage expanding and contracting as it breathed at the end of my bed in the light of the moon. It startled me so badly I shot up out of bed, gasping for air, waking my girlfriend at the same time. Of course, upon my rising, the thing vanished. She asked me what was wrong, and upon telling her, she didn't seem fazed. I mean, why would she be, she'd gotten used to my 'happenings'.

I could go on and on and keep detailing my encounters, but I won't, as most are similar to what I've already mentioned. What I really wanted to stress by contributing to this book was that I believe two things: one, that someone who suffers trauma at a young age can be opened to seeing or experiencing paranormal activity, and two, a person themselves can be haunted. Now I don't want people to think by hanging out with me or simply being in my presence you'll experience anything; it's more that I'm now attracted to such things or at the minimum more aware. All in all, my life seems to never be a bore, and no matter where I go, I can always find something lurking there, from shadow people, orbs, weird gray/white humanoids and so forth. I don't think I'll ever be at peace, and you know what, I don't know if I want to stop having these experiences. What I would like, though, is to stop being woken from a good night's rest.

GHOST HUNTING WILL BE FUN, THEY SAID

*R*umors can run rampant as to why a location has various activity and numerous entities inhabiting it. In this case, a workplace is home to children's laughter, moving furniture, a disembodied limb, black mists, and more. A place like this is a veritable gold mine of potential evidence and interactions for 'ghost hunters'. As Sarah proves, we are often told to be careful what we wish for…as the excitement of an investigation turns into a very scary confirmation experience.

***

I know this sounds cliché, but I began my

quest for answers into the paranormal phenomenon when I started experiencing strange happenings in my childhood home.

From an early age, I saw shadows in the hallways, items being tossed, the drapes on our window move as if someone had pulled on them from the inside, and a battery-powered doll that would sit up on its own and sing.

I was never really scared except for the one time I saw a shadow figure. It was completely black, stood about six feet tall, and appeared to be wearing a long black hood and robe. The misty and distorted figure had no legs, but it was there, as it covered the pictures in the hallway. As I stared at it, my terror was palpable, and to this day I'm glad it never looked back at me. Just as quickly as I noticed it, it disappeared.

But it is not that encounter that I am here to tell. No, the story I want to share happened when I went to work at a reopened banquet facility near Pittsburgh, Pennsylvania. I'd heard rumors about the place being very haunted, with some employees refusing to go back to work after seeing a ghostly figure of a woman float down a ramp in the kitchen. Even my mother's best friend told me she and others were pushed out of the elevators the second the door would open. The strange occurrences got so bad that the management had a priest come to bless the building. But even after hearing all these rumors and stories, I thought they were just trying to scare me.

Well, it did not take long after I started to work there that I discovered for myself just how haunted the place really was. I was in a supply closet, grabbing cleaning supplies, when I heard the distinct voice of a woman say my name. It was so clear that I thought it was my co-worker, so I yelled out, "I'm in here getting cleaning supplies!"

Twenty seconds later, I heard the same female voice call my name again. However, this time I was able to pick up on more details in the voice. I could tell it was an older woman, so out of an abundance of caution for my co-worker, I left the closet to see if she was okay or needed anything. I looked on the first floor for her, but she wasn't there. I then proceeded upstairs to the second floor. As I walked past the windows, I looked out and saw my co-worker on her hands and knees, pulling weeds by the sign for the banquet facility. Seeing her out there didn't make sense to me. How could she be out there so quickly?

I ran out and asked what she needed, to which she replied, "I didn't need anything." I told her I had heard her calling me, and she said she was out there for maybe half an hour, pulling weeds and planting flowers. I didn't know what to think, but I know what I heard, and it was most definitely a woman's voice calling my name.

After that on numerous occasions I heard kids laughing near the elevator adjacent to the same supply closet where I had heard the woman's voice. Hearing the laughter of the children unnerved me a little.

I ended up working there for a few years until they again closed it down. During my tenure, I saw many strange and unusual things, such as objects moving: like our place settings would be set; then the next morning they'd be somewhere else. We'd have furniture move, and even some people saw manifestations. One night I even saw a black mist forming. I literally have so many stories that I could fill a book like this with them.

After the facility closed, a group of us thought it would be fun to conduct our own ghost-hunting research. Armed with a handheld voice recorder, flashlights, a video recorder, and a handheld picture camera, we went on the hunt for ghosts.

The five of us started our ghost-hunting adventure in the event room upstairs. It was a big room with smaller adjacent rooms where the table and chairs were stored. It was those smaller rooms where I was always left with a heavy and uneasy feeling. It was so bad I never wanted to go in there unless someone came with me. Our plan when we arrived in the room was to just talk to whatever spirits might be there.

After huddling around in a circle, we began to ask whatever was there to show itself and give us a sign. One woman in our group said she could see someone in her third eye, standing in the corner. I forgot to mention, part of our agreement was that we'd share with each other whatever thoughts or feelings we had.

As the woman shared her thoughts, I couldn't stop staring at a particular spot in the room. I was transfixed on it; all my focus and attention poured into it so much that I couldn't move. My focus was broken when another girl with us jumped to her feet and in a panic raced from the room, saying that she had to leave.

It was at that moment I looked back at the spot and became filled with dread and knew something very tall was behind me, like an ominous totem hovering and ready to do me harm. I wanted to speak but found I was unable to; it was as if I was in a trance. A rage began to build in me. As I looked at my companions, the desire to lash out at them grew, but even with those thoughts I was unable to move. I tried in vain to move but couldn't. A pressure rose in my body so much that I wanted to jump out of my skin. Suddenly, the right side of my mouth curled up into a grin, sort of like how the Grinch smiles. It was a devilish grin and not welcome. I wanted to stop, but I wasn't in control.

A deep sense of fear rose alongside the rage. I yelled in my head for it to stop, but it did not. Finally, I was able to move and took immediate action. I sprang to my feet and sprinted out of the room, down the hall towards the stairs. With panic fueling my every step, I raced down the stairwell, skipping steps until I reached the first floor. I turned in the direction of the lobby and didn't stop until I reached it.

I was out of breath and my lungs burned. I

dropped to my knees, as I felt weak, and that was when I noticed the girl who had run out earlier sitting stoically on the lobby piano bench with her head in her trembling hands.

"Are you okay?" I asked.

She told me that when she was in the room, she'd felt someone standing over her and she couldn't move.

Her words hit me like a ton of bricks, as she'd just explained the exact same feeling or sense that I had.

What really freaked me out was when she used her finger to curl up her right lip. That was enough for me; I didn't need to hear more. I stood up and walked away without telling her I had experienced the EXACT same thing.

We were by no means professional ghost hunters, but watching television, I learned to make sure to go over the video recording and pictures of that night with an eye to debunk anything that had a possibility of being explained, but what we had caught in the pictures made me a TRUE believer.

In numerous shots we had orbs that appeared to be emitting light and had a solid border around them with maybe two or three transparent ones. Another picture showed what I believe to this day to be a woman's face. She had a long nose, and her hair hung down to her shoulders and was all one length. Another picture terrified me because it appeared as if her face turned into a skeleton face. Then finally the one picture that sealed the deal on me never going back again came from upstairs outside the table and chair room. In the photograph you can clearly see a transparent mist orb with a face! Yes, there is no doubt what you see in the image is a man's face and what appears to be him wearing a tall top hat similar to one worn by Abraham Lincoln. What added to the creepiness of the photo was the face clearly has a nose, eyes, with an open-mouthed sinister grin, and the teeth were filed to points. I just knew upon laying eyes on it that this had been the thing standing over me in the room.

The only thing we caught on the voice recorder, which I was not present for, came downstairs in the bar area. On the recording we clearly heard three people talking, but we know this wasn't us, as we weren't there. When I listened to the recording on the headphones, I heard my name being said. At first, I wasn't sure, but I listened to it over and over and had my friends listen to it too without telling them what I heard. It was unanimous; they all could hear my name being said.

I never went back to the banquet facility ever again, but I don't look upon it as a negative experience, as I learned a lot. First, I think I now understand why I feel spirits and sometimes see them; it's because I have empathic abilities and have a connection to environmental energy. As far as the spirits in the facility, I know there are three women and a man. One woman knows that she is dead but is stuck. One is residual energy that travels by the elevator to the ramp in the kitchen—she does this over and over; back and forth she goes—and lastly the one upstairs. She is a very nurturing spirit, likes to hum nursery hymns, like a mother would to their infant to get them to sleep. I can't tell if she is residual or not for some reason, but I do wonder if it's the evil man who holds her there.

The EVIL man is a puzzle to me. There was an instance that a child came up to us, crying, and told us a man upstairs scared him. He had been playing with his cars right outside the table room. Only weeks later did we ask him about it again, to which he said, "Yeah, I 'member him." We asked if the man said anything to him, and his reply was, "Yeah, his name was NUMBER 6." I freaked out because I know when demons are asked their names, especially in exorcisms, they sometimes state the number of demons inside the person, hence NUMBER 6. I don't know if this was a demon that had possessed this man while he was living and has not let him go, or maybe the demon is being a trickster. No matter what it is, it scared me enough to stop my investigating.

Ghost hunting would be fun, they said...but it turned out to be one of the most terrifying nights of my life.

IT WOULD COME AT NIGHT

I'm sure most of you know my very own shadow person experience; if not, you can read about it in BEYOND THE FRAY: BIGFOOT and even find it on my website. I'm not alone in experiencing such things and can confirm just how scary coming face-to-face with one of them can be.

When I heard from John about his experiences, specifically about the shadow person, which would come 'home' each night, I got a chill that ran down my spine. There's just something very creepy and out of sorts about a shadow person, and I hope if you haven't seen one, that you never do.

***

I worked in law enforcement for many years, and the incidents I'm about to share occurred during this time. This is why I won't detail where this happened, as I would rather not deal with any of the blowback from it.

The second I moved into the old single-level, two-bedroom house, I could sense something about it. I'm sure it could have been the age, the house was about seventy years old, but maybe it had something to do with how it looked. The house was near a flood plain and was built on stilts, making the front door about twelve feet off the ground. The area flooded a lot, especially during the rainy season, so we'd prep the house to weather the raging storms we'd have during this time. This included placing thick plastic sheeting across the windows to protect them from flying debris, more about how this is important later.

I had a roommate at the time; he lived in the back bedroom, while I had the front bedroom. The house itself had a weird floor plan. My bedroom connected directly to the kitchen but also had a door to the outside. If you exited my room into the kitchen, the next room was a dining space where the front door was, and to the left of that was a large living room and just beyond the second bedroom.

It wasn't days after arriving did things happen; however, at the time I didn't know what they were. My roommate was also in law enforcement and at the time worked a different shift than me. Several times per week the door in my bedroom that led to the outside would open. I'd hear someone walk through my room into the kitchen, turn on the lights, then proceed through the house, in each room turning on the lights, then the television, and go into the back bedroom. I kept thinking it was my roommate being a bit rude until I decided I had had enough. I went back to his room, knocked on the door, and told him to stop, but he didn't reply. I opened his door to discover he wasn't there. I was instantly freaked and questioned if I'd actually heard it and seen the lights come on. I was in disbelief and decided then to just ignore it. I turned off the lights and went to sleep.

A week went by and nothing else happened until the night I heard the knocking. I'd come home from having a couple of beers with friends. I sat up in front of the television and watched until I fell asleep. I was awoken by knocking on the front door in the dining space. The top of the door had glass panes, and the knocks were more like heavy taps on the glass. I got up to go see who it could be. I turned on the outside light and looked out, but no one was there. I shrugged it off as nothing and went back to lie down on the couch and watch television again, as now I was awake. I should note that my roommate was out of town at this time.

Not a minute after turning on the television, I heard the tapping on the front door again. Annoyed, I got up, went to the front door, and turned on the lights, but this time I threw open the door.

There was no one there. I was shocked because if this were kids playing a prank, they'd have to race down the stairs and run off to hide. Either way, I wasn't convinced it was something paranormal, so I hollered for whoever it was to stop because I was a cop. After a solid minute, I turned off the light, locked the door, and went back to the couch. This time I was focused on the front door, ready to pounce the second I heard a creak on the stairs.

My focus was shattered when I heard tapping on the window to my left. I wasn't just annoyed now, I was angry. I shot up, ran to the door, threw it open and raced down the stairs; the entire time I hollered that I'd find them. I made a hard turn left at the base of the stair and rounded the side of the house and stopped in shock when I saw the window is a good fifteen feet off the ground. My anger turned to an uneasiness. I looked all around, but nothing was there, except I could now feel something. I hurried back inside, locked the door, and called it a night by going to my room. I heard nothing else the rest of the night.

A few weeks later I was awoken by the sound of my outside door opening. This time I jumped out of bed to find out what it could be or catch my roommate being a rude idiot. I stepped into the bedroom/kitchen doorway and saw a silhouette of a person in the dining room; they were tall, almost hitting the ceiling. I knew by looking at its size that it wasn't my roommate. Goosebumps exploded all over my body. I stepped back into my room and went to my nightstand; in the drawer I kept my service pistol. I pulled it out and went back to the doorway to find the shadow figure still there, the ambient light of the half-moon illuminating behind it enough so I could make it out. I didn't raise my pistol, but I had it at the ready while I reached in and turned on the light. I flipped the switch and the thing vanished. I immediately searched the house, but found no one or any sign that anyone had come in. What made this even more odd was my outside door was unlocked. I didn't leave it that way; I'm very conscious about security, so whatever it was, it had the ability to unlock the door.

I later moved my bed over and slid the nightstand in front of the door. After that the door never opened again, but I would still hear sounds, walking, tapping, and lights would turn on and off. When my lease ended, I couldn't wait to leave, and I still don't know to this day what it was I saw until I heard someone mention shadow people. I have to guess that's what it was, but I don't know why it was there or what it wanted.

THE WAR NEVER ENDED

ain and suffering, that is one explanation for the existence of spirits and paranormal activity in a certain location. The greater the pain, suffering and death, the higher the chance of the location being haunted. With that logic, it makes sense that battlefields are a prime location to spot and witness ghostly apparitions, some seemingly caught in a loop, repeating the horrific experiences that led to their demise.

One such place exists in Southern Maryland; there a small and beautiful peninsula was converted to a prisoner of war camp during the American Civil War. Since the war ended, Point Lookout has been known as a hot spot for paranormal activity, with many visitors and employees of the park reporting countless sightings.

Geoff was one such employee who not only worked at the state park, which now occupies the area that was once the prison camp, but also lived there. In the short three months he spent at the state park, he experienced numerous encounters with the unexplained and can say with conviction that the ghosts of Point Lookout aren't just stories to frighten people and attract curious onlookers, they are real and everywhere.

***

I had just graduated high school and had seven months before I shipped off to recruit training in the Marine Corps. Not wanting to just sit around, I put out feelers for a job. Lo and behold, my older brother worked as a ranger at Point Lookout State Park in Maryland and said he could help to get me a job at the park, at least through the high-traffic months of the summer. I jumped at the opportunity, applied, and within a couple of weeks I had a position working in the campground office. There I'd be registering campers and doing odd jobs here and there. One nice benefit I had was I could live with my brother and another ranger in the park. The accommodations weren't plush, but for an eighteen-year-old guy it was perfect.

The house we lived in wasn't really a house, just a large single-room cinder-block building, which we partitioned off with wall lockers. I didn't have a bed, but a cot; but like I said, I was eighteen and didn't care. This was going to be a fun time living with my older brother, whom I got along with, and was the first time I'd be living away from home.

I was aware of the paranormal activity at the park, as my brother, John, had told me all about it, not just his experiences but others he'd heard about. I was fascinated and I'll admit that part of my excitement about living in the park had to do with that. Having the chance to live in a haunted area seemed really cool.

Before Point Lookout was a state park, it had the notorious history of being the largest and one of the deadliest prison camps run by the Union during the Civil War, not as bad as Andersonville in the South, but not far behind. At the height of the war in late 1863, it held over twenty thousand Confederate prisoners, although it was only suited to adequately sustain ten thousand. The conditions were poor and resulted in thousands of deaths due to disease and lack of proper nutrition. It's these numbers of deaths and suffering that many believe is the catalyst for so much activity in the area.

I hadn't spent a night there before I had my first experience. My brother, John, our roommate, and a fellow ranger, Jaime, and I were sitting the living room, having a beer, when suddenly the front door of the place creaked open. Jaime's dog, Roscoe, an Irish setter, jumped to his feet, hair raised, and began to growl in the direction of the front door.

I was on the left side of the couch, John on the right, and Jaime was sitting in a cushioned armchair opposite us. I looked at John and asked, "What's going on?"

John took a swig of beer, smiled and calmly answered, "We have a visitor." A slight grin was stretched across his face, mainly because he was anxious to see how I responded.

I sat up, beer in hand, and gulped. Now, I'd had other types of experiences before, but this still had me a bit on edge. Was this visitor good, bad, or just one that is on a repeating loop?

Roscoe kept growling and his head pivoted as if he could see the thing. He turned his head enough to the right until he was staring directly in between John and me on the couch.

I scooted as close as I could get to the left arm of the couch and in a vain attempt strained my eyes with hopes of seeing anything, but alas, I couldn't; however, Roscoe could and he was standing guard, hair still raised and his deep guttural growl signaling to all of us just how upset he was.

A minute went by; then Roscoe slowly started to track something back towards the front door, his eyes glued on whatever he could see until the front door moved. A second after that, Roscoe calmed down and went back to lying on the floor.

"It's gone?" I asked.

"Yeah," John replied, again taking a swig of beer.

I had goosebumps all over. This was thrilling. *How cool was that?* I thought to myself. This was going to be the best summer I'd ever had.

The days turned to weeks with me working long hours, mainly night shift at the camp office, with minimal ghostly experiences. Yes, I'd see doors slam or items go missing; but what I wanted to have was something more profound. I wanted to see something, a true manifestation. I never got that, but I got close; in fact, it was very close.

Like I said, I'd been given the night shift at the camp office. What this meant was I closed the office near midnight then was tasked with being a glorified janitor—that's a lie, I was *the* janitor.

I can't remember what night it was, but I feel this was near the middle of summer, like in July. I had locked down the camp office that night but hadn't been tasked with any cleaning. With no cleaning responsibilities, I could relax until my shift ended in the morning. My night was ruined when Mike, the ranger on shift, showed up in the patrol car. He had a job for me, and it was janitorial, of course.

He needed me to clean what they called the Beach House. This was a building on the river side of the peninsula and fronted the beach there. Inside the Beach House were bathrooms, showers and changing stalls.

We pulled up just outside the painted cinder-block structure. A lonely sconce outside the entrance provided the only light around.

Mike turned to me, handed me a radio and a flashlight, and gave me instructions on what needed to be done.

I nodded and opened the door. Just as I stepped out, he stopped me.

"Now if you need me or you want to leave, just hit me on the radio," he said.

"Okay," I replied and closed the door.

Mike pulled away, leaving me standing there staring at the entrance of the Beach House. Behind me I could hear the subtle sound of the tide coming in, and the smell of the river hit my nose and engaged those senses.

I took a deep breath and, with keys in hand, headed for the women's entrance first. I unlocked it, reached my hand around the corner, and turned on the light switch.

The fluorescent bulbs crackled and popped to life.

The inside was shaped like a U. If you stood in the doorway and looked straight ahead, you'd be looking at a cinder-block wall. Turn right and then make an immediate left, you'd walk past a series of changing stalls. Turn left then make an immediate right, you'd run into about a dozen toilet stalls. If you followed either way, they made their way around and to a communal shower in between. In the back of the building was a supply closet. I made my way there, unlocked it and removed a bucket, filled it with warm water and shoved in a mop. I found another bucket and placed toilet bowl cleaner, paper towels and Windex in it. As the mop soaked, I went to work on cleaning the toilets first.

I was bent over, scrubbing away, when I heard the front door swing open. I stood and listened.

On the opposite side where the changing stalls were, I heard the distinct sound of hard sole shoes crunching sand into the ceramic tile floor. One footfall after another crunched as whoever it was made their slow procession towards the shower.

A spike of fear rose in me. Unsure of what else to do, I called out, "Who's there?"

No response. The footsteps had stopped when I called out.

I dropped the scrubber and grabbed the long Maglite flashlight I had, not to use for light, but as a club if I needed it. "Hello, who's there?"

Still no response.

Nervous, I made my way around until I was at the end of the changing stall area. I walked up to one, took hold of the shower curtain covering, and pulled it aside. No one there. I went to the next, then the next. I stopped halfway and thought that my actions reminded me of a character in a horror movie who was about to be killed by the serial killer. What didn't make sense was I'd heard the steps stop about where I was, yet there was no one there. I completed looking in the other stalls but found no sign of anyone. I shrugged and began to question if I'd even heard it.

I went back to the toilet and started to work again. Not ten seconds went by when I froze. My sixth sense told me right then that someone was standing behind me. I could literally feel them almost pressing down on me. I was bent down scrubbing the toilet, but I couldn't find the courage to stand up or look back. I just knew if I did that, I'd be staring into the face of something sinister.

I pressed my eyes closed, took a gulp, and ever so slowly began to crane my head back to look, but stopped when I could feel that whoever it was now stood inches from my face.

I was in terror, pure terror. I shook my head and loudly said, "No!" This was my way of telling whatever it was that I would not be intimidated. I stood up, spun around and again barked, "No!"

Now facing out, I saw no one, but I could still feel a presence of some sort. I was done; I couldn't stay there any longer. I snatched the radio from my hip, keyed it and made a call for Mike to come pick me up.

Mike replied that he was on his way.

I took everything to the supply closet, tossed it in, locked it up and raced out. As soon as I locked the door, I saw the headlights from the patrol car come around the corner. I breathed a sigh of relief and rushed towards it.

I got in the car, my face flush and my voice showing signs of stress.

With a grin stretched across his face, Mike asked, "You saw something, didn't you?"

"No, but something was there."

"I know, why do you think I had you come down to clean it? I'll never go in there again."

I returned Mike's comment with a disappointed smirk.

The rest of my days at the park weren't as eventful as that one night, but I had more unique experiences.

My story isn't to stop people from visiting the park. On the contrary, the park is a beautiful place, rich in nature and history, but also has its share of paranormal activity. So if you ever make your way there, enjoy yourself, but don't be too shocked if you happen to see a ghost or get a chill run down your spine for no apparent reason at all.

THE FARMHOUSE

A *farmhouse in California, built in 1931 which also happens to sit on the Pony Express Trail, is host to seemingly highly intelligent entities. And this is not a 'classic' haunting scenario by any means. What starts as strange feelings in certain parts of the home moves to seeing small beings, hearing disembodied voices, and even strange prints going up walls. And this is just the beginning.*

***

I think it best to give a bit of history about the house where I had my experiences growing up. The house was a two-story farmhouse built in 1931. It was constructed well with redwood beams throughout but needed updating. It had no insulation, no central heating system, and you could see where each room had wood-burning stoves at one time, as the holes for the chimney pipes were still visible. The garage was detached, and there were two rooms in the back of it with no doors on them. The first time I laid eyes on the garage, I found it eerie. The house was in the suburbs of a city I won't name, but it's in Sacramento County, California. The lot was large; like most around were, it was near the top of a hill and was zoned for livestock, so many neighbors had a horse or mule. The idea my parents had for getting the house was to make it a hobby farm for me and my sister.

This house wasn't the oldest by any means, as I recall an old Victorian house at the top of the hill had been built in the 1860s. In fact, the Pony Express line ran through that house's property, and the house there had been used as a staging ground, and there was even an old school there.

I moved into the house with my mom, stepdad, and little stepsister, in January of 1988, making me about nine years old. It wasn't long after we moved in did I meet the neighbors who too had lived in the house. One of the first things their kids, who were a bit younger, said was that the house was haunted. I found that odd and shrugged it off as them just trying to scare me.

My room was upstairs on the south side of the house. I remember clearly the first thing that I felt when I moved my stuff into the room was in the closet and in a built-in desk area. I don't know how else to explain, but it felt like a bad lie. Like someone had done something awfully bad and had hidden something there, and now there was a residual effect from it.

We all eventually got settled in, and I went to school. One of the first things I experienced was seeing something in my peripheral vision. I'd do my homework at the desk, and from it you could see the stairs. Countless times I'd see something in my peripheral vision walk up the stairs. I'd go to look fully, and it would be gone. This happened so often that I'd try to stare at it without looking completely, but it still knew I was looking at it and disappear. The thing looked like an evil leprechaun. I'm not saying it was that, just that if I have to describe it for people to get an image, that's what it looked like. It was about knee high, thin, and it would always give me a devilish smile. I swear it was there to taunt me, nothing more.

Before I go into and detail other experiences, let me say that there were a lot, and without a doubt some could find scientific explanations, but for the most part the overwhelming evidence I'll detail will show the house had many entities, with some of them probably being demonic. The house itself was just an unsettling place, and a heaviness was felt all around.

Around the three-month mark of being in the house, I woke to the sound of a child's voice coming from the area of the stairs. It kept repeatedly saying the word *awd*. The voice would rise and fall in pitch and increase and decrease in speed. I got so scared, I jumped from my bed and raced to my parents' room to sleep with them. This wasn't something I'd do; in fact, I never slept with my parents until that night.

Something that I have to mention now is whatever was in the house, it would mimic us. No matter who was there, it would trick us by speaking like others in the family, and I know this will sound strange, but it was aware of holidays. This tells me now that it was an intelligent presence. To illustrate it was aware of holidays, I'll tell you this story. It was Easter of 1988 and my stepdad had painted the walls white. Looking back, I'd say having white walls and kids isn't a good idea, but that's what he did. Well, it was Easter like I said, my sister was hunting Easter eggs, and at the base of the stairs and at the landing midway up, my stepdad found rabbit paw prints on the walls.

He believed it was me and got mad, but I hadn't done it. I can forgive him for thinking it was me because what else in his mind could explain it? I never imagined it was my little sister, because she was the opposite of doing such things, and it wasn't like she knew I was having these experiences and was tricking me. In fact, it wasn't a couple of months later that she had her own.

It was now the summer. My sister's room was downstairs at the front of the house, giving her a view of the driveway and garage. She woke to a bright light coming through the blinds of her window. She got up, peeked out, and saw before her a clown facing the garage, juggling balls. Not a second after seeing it, the clown faced her, dropped the balls, and waved. Terrified, she jumped back in her bed and covered herself with the blankets. She told me about it, but I dismissed it even though I'd had my own unique things happening. What's really creepy is she went outside the next day to where she saw the clown and found one of the balls feet away in the garden; neither one of us knew whose ball it was. Even to this day my sister swears she saw it and wasn't asleep or dreaming.

It needs to be said before I go on that the events in the house didn't happen on a daily basis. There would be long stretches of time where I'd see or hear nothing, but one thing that we all felt, and my mom even agreed, and that was we always felt a heaviness about the house and that someone was always watching us.

Speaking of my mom, she too would experience things, mainly electrical disturbances like lamps turning on and off or the television changing channels. I too experienced the electrical anomalies and still wonder if it had something to do with the house being old.

My mom also heard voices, and like I said, it would mimic us. For instance, my stepsister was at her mom's house one weekend, but I still heard her voice call my name. Forgetting she was gone, I went to her room to find her not there. My mom also heard my voice call her; thing is, I was gone. I don't know why it would do that, but it's creepy when you hear a family member call out your name only to find out they're not there.

As the years went on, the events continued, but like I said, they'd sometimes be spaced out by weeks and months. When I was thirteen, my mom was pregnant and would eventually give birth to my half-sister. Even she would end up seeing things when she was a bit older.

My half-sister had friends over, but that didn't stop her from seeing what she thought was one of them run upstairs, only to find out her friend was still downstairs in the kitchen with her mom.

One of the creepiest things happened to my mom after I had moved out. She told me that she exited the bathroom to find a towering shadow person standing in the hallway in front of her. It was black, void of light, and stood two feet taller than her. Of course, she was alarmed but wasn't going to let it scare her. Being my mom, the ever-polite person, she said, "Excuse me," and then proceeded to walk through it and down the hall. While she disregarded it at the time, I believe that was the last straw for her, as they started to look for a new house.

Even my stepdad wasn't immune. Now, he never said he'd seen anything, and I can't ask him, as he passed away years ago. But what he told me only confirms there was something in the house. I had moved out, but he said something that still to this day gives me chills. He told me that a couple of Mormon missionaries stopped by. My stepdad was Mormon too, so he opened the door and invited them in; however, the two missionaries quickly retracted their offer to speak. Struck by the refusal to come inside, my stepdad stood dumbfounded. The missionaries told him that they couldn't come in because there was something evil in the house. They promptly turned and left. When I heard that, I got creeped out, but mainly because I had lived there for so long.

I can go on and on about the house and the property, but I won't, as the stories and experiences are numerous. I wonder now after all these years and have even recently spoken at length with my mom about them, what was there, and was it tied to the house or the property in general? I know we'd see things outside as well as inside. From the creepy clown to explosions in the back field. There was something on that property. Even our neighbors had their own experiences as far as seeing things like the explosion.

I hated that house, and if it burned to the ground, I'd be fine with that. I live about twenty minutes from there and recently saw it from the road. On the outside the house is quaint and charming, but I know on the inside it is nothing like that. Since I moved out over twenty years ago, I personally haven't had any other type of paranormal event or activity, and

I'm glad of that. After living in that house for ten years, I had enough experiences to last several lifetimes.

DEVIATUS

*F*or a short period of time, Jeremy Enfinger's drive to work also brought with it several sightings of a very tall, black-hooded figure on rooftops and even atop fifty-foot-tall light poles. Curiosity towards this entity turned to fear when its full attention settled on him. As we continued to talk, we soon learned Jeremy has had other experiences as well.

***

I've had personal experiences with the paranormal throughout my life. I work in the medical field and tend to keep quiet about these encounters to protect my standing in this field. Many people in the medical community frown upon these sorts of things, and you're likely to get more than one crazy look if it comes up. A couple of outlets I utilized were producing and hosting two different shows in the paranormal and horror genres...one called *Deviatus*...and the other most recent one, *The Storage Papers*.

In 2004, right after my wife and I married and we had our first child, we moved to Mesa, Arizona. Our daughter was up a lot at night, which meant we were up a lot as well. She was also having some medical issues, so that compounded the situation. On the way home from work one day—this was about 4:30 in the afternoon—I saw something off to the right, in my periphery. I look over, and off in the distance, about eighty to a hundred yards away, a very tall black figure was standing atop the roof of a house. I brushed it off as nothing. An early adornment of a Halloween decoration or something of the like. I watched it closely as I passed. It stood at least eight feet tall and was hooded, but without an opening at the front. At about the time I'm going to fully write it off and forget about it...it crouches down. This was no decoration, and it totally freaked me out.

Over the period of the following two weeks, I saw this tall intimidating figure three or four more times. Each time, it was in a different location...but within the same square mile of town. After the third time, I thought to bring a camera with me. So two weeks later I spot it again and attempt to slow down a bit on the freeway while fiddling with the camera to get it on, prompting honks from my fellow drivers...but when I looked back, it had disappeared. Well, doesn't that just figure, right? I turn the camera off and set it back down on the seat next to me. I look back up (my speed getting back up to normal), and on top of one of the fifty-foot-tall light poles that adorn the side of the freeway was another one of these things. Or maybe the same one? It's crouched down, and its head is turning because it's following me with its gaze. It scared me enough to where I was ducking down inside my truck while trying to look around at other drivers. Did they see it? I could tell they didn't because they were only looking at me and my odd driving behavior.

I went home and told my wife about it, and the concern was great enough that I went to see a psychologist about it. They ran some lab work and asked many questions. I had no history of depression or anxiety, which I didn't, but what I did have was some sleep deprivation around that time because of what was going on with my daughter. They labeled it hallucinations brought on by sleep deprivation. I admit that it very well could have been that, but the argument against this diagnosis is the fact that this was years ago, and I have been sleep-deprived, really, ever since, even still getting up a couple of times a night to administer medicine to my kids. After the incident with it watching me while atop the light pole...I never saw it again.

The very first paranormal experience I had

was around the age of ten. We lived in a house in Flagstaff, Arizona, for only a few months and were in fact in the process of loading a moving van. We had one more night to sleep in the home and get up early and start driving. Mom, my stepdad and I were all set up to sleep on a queen mattress in the living room. It was a cold night, and even though we had a fire going that night...I woke around 2:30 a.m., freezing. I looked up to see a shadow figure with red eyes walking past the fireplace. I remember this vividly because I could not see the fire through this figure's legs. It walked past the fire, ignoring me...only looking forward, turning right to make its way down the hall and turning into one of the rooms. This happened to be my (former) room. I must have jumped or made a noise because I startled everyone else awake, only to have my stepdad ask, "Did you see it?" I replied that I had, and he proceeded to tell me that they'd been seeing that walk into my room every night.

That next day, during the drive to California, we spoke about the goings-on in that home. I was a latch-key kid, with both parents working long hours. I would be the last one to leave the house in the morning, and the first one home in the afternoon. Often, I would come home and all the cabinets and drawers in the kitchen would be flung wide open, with all the lights on in the entire house. We had an extremely sweet and mellow Doberman pinscher, and I'd go looking for her to take her on a walk. On two occasions, I found her shivering in a corner, and when I approached her, she would snap viciously at the air.

My mom leaned toward the shadow figure being a human spirit...why, I'm not sure. She would also hear voices and knocking on the walls...mostly while I was sleeping. She also admitted that the dog would sometimes refuse to go to specific areas in the home, but only at certain times.

Before I moved to the home I'm in now,

my wife and I had a number of experiences, but interestingly it was only after new neighbors moved in. It was mostly whispering or voices, but at one point my wife and I had a shared experience where we had two vastly different perceptions of what happened. The kids were in bed, and we were out in the living room, watching TV. With my kids not sleeping much, we had the volume down extremely low and the closed-captions on.

I looked over towards the kitchen and saw something coming from the ceiling that looked to me like a wadded-up black T-shirt. As it dropped to the floor, it changed shape and vanished. At the very moment it hit the floor, my wife, who wasn't in the room to witness this, said she heard a loud bang.

I didn't hear any sound at all. So I got the visual experience, while she got the audio. Very odd to say the least, and I have no clue what that was. We walked over to inspect the area but could find no evidence of anything ever being there.

My grandmother is one hundred percent Native American, and in fact, she's one of the few remaining members of the Creek Nation Tribe in Florida. She currently lives in Los Angeles County.

I always noticed peculiar things about her during my early years. Like one time she asked me to get her a cup of iced tea in her large glass. As I reached for a tall yellow plastic cup, she said, "No, not that one, the one next to it."

What made this so odd was she wasn't in the room. How could she see what cup I was reaching for? There were other little things she would do that told me she was very in tune with the world around her.

I've also been out on paranormal investigations with 'ghost hunting' groups. I had interviewed a couple of the guys from this team for my podcast, and they invited me out with them. We went to Pioneer Park in downtown San Diego, which has an extremely interesting history. It used to be a cemetery, with some of the headstones left in the back portion of it. It was being neglected, so the city took over in the early '80s, getting rid of most of the headstones, and put a park over it. Unbeknownst to many, there are over eight hundred bodies still interred within. One within the group said she's 'sensitive', which made me instantly skeptical. At some point during the night I saw something duck behind a tree that was situated behind her. I was about to say something when she said, "There's someone right behind me." That was impressive.

After all I've experienced personally and researched for my podcasts, I've tried to retain my skepticism. It is often easy to be led in one way of thinking versus another. I will say that I feel there are many possibilities as to what we may be interacting with. Even when we don't want to.

FEAR THE REAPER

*B*rian *has seen and been part of many strange occurrences. From disconnected phones ringing with static on the other end after answering, and even residual energies strong enough to include multiple voices in an empty kitchen. And ever wondered what was in the air vent above you? Well, Brian has an idea...and it wouldn't be something you'd hope to see. But not all experiences were negative or scary. Some were absolutely miraculous.*

***

I have had many things happen in my lifetime that range from scary to incredible...even bordering on a miracle. My first memory of something strange was being in a crib in our first home. I don't know if I was even two years old at this point, but I vividly remember looking through the bars of the crib with the door being left cracked open, as my mom had left it...but as soon as she would leave the room, I saw a shadow come out of the closet. It would always move towards the doorway where the light would come in, and completely blot out the light. It would then make its way over to my crib and emit a deep growl. I would of course cry, bringing my mom abruptly back in. This only happened a handful of times, but this was my inception into the world of the paranormal.

We now fast-forward to my third-grade school year, and we moved to a home that was comprised of all brick, settled on a beautiful acre lot. We lived there until I was a senior in high school. It was originally intended as a duplex, so each side mirrored the other in design...but they subsequently tore out the middle wall, making it a single-family home.

My bedroom ended up being where one of the kitchens had stood, and in fact the gas stove was still in there, which I loved as a kid...you know, experiments! Another item in the room was an old phone, guessing from the '50s...an old rotary phone, adorned with cloth over the cord. It was not connected to the wall, but when I would go into the room, it would ring. At one point I decided to answer it. And as if its ringing wasn't amazing enough, there was static on the other end with what sounded like a voice attempting to come through. It then went dead, and that was when I decided the phone needed a new place to sit. So out to the shed it went.

On many a night, I would wake to a noise coming from the other end of the house. I usually tried to ignore it and go back to sleep, but once...I decided to go investigate. I made my way to the working kitchen, to see the door closed, but the light on, and sounds of a full-blown party emanating from within. People talking, plates and glasses clanking, etc. I opened the door…and it was pitch black. Silent. With not a soul inside.

My sister Beth told me that some nights her bed would move around the room. Actually…the word she utilized was float. And, as if what I've already mentioned wasn't enough…occasionally all of the doorknobs (inside and outside) would shake violently, and then suddenly go still. My mother also admitted that there were things that happened in that home to her that really disturbed her, but she would not put more words to it than that. I will say that the activity died down tremendously as Beth and I aged…so I'm left wondering if we somehow created some, or even all of it ourselves.

This next event caused a change in me that turned out to be incredibly positive. It was profound. We were still living in the duplex house, and I would walk to and from school. There was a large lot that I would walk through to go to school. There was a large German shepherd across the street from the lot. It would be left out front, unchained…and the yard was not fenced in. This dog absolutely loved to chase me. And it made a point to bark and growl every time it did it. This was my route to and from school, so to go around meant a huge addition to my trek.

On one day…well, let's just say it wasn't a good one. I was in a foul mood. I decided to walk closer than usual to the ill-tempered dog, not caring of the consequences. In true form, the dog was there and ready to do our usual dance. Now, I was a tall, skinny kid at this point and I had the mentality of *screw it…I'm going to break anything in my way, in half.* The chase started, and I admittedly broke down. I started crying, running…and he was right behind me. Well…something inside me completely snapped. I whirled around to face my pursuer. A huge roar came out of me, unlike anything I'd ever been able to produce before. Something that didn't even sound human. I even held up my hands like claws, to enhance the effect. The dog lost all purpose and fire (held steady for months on end), yelps…and runs all the way home. It never bothered me again. My summation of this incident is that my truest, highest self-took over and cut through the fear.

So switching gears and time periods…there was a point in my life that I felt a pull to be in the ministry. Since then, my belief system has changed, but for four years, I was a volunteer chaplain at a juvenile institution. I was all in, and it was very meaningful to me. During this time though, much of the paranormal activity I had almost gotten used to as a child started ramping up. At one point, I was downtown doing street ministry sessions. I would talk to homeless people, get them food, or even bring them home with me to try to aid them in their situation.

Once, I was out for ministry purposes with a friend of mine. He happened to be an exceptionally large man, a bodybuilder in fact. He would often accompany me on my outings.

One night extremely late, probably around 1 a.m., there was a kid out and about. He looked to be about twelve years old. With concern for his safety, we offered to walk him home, as this was not a good part of town. He for some reason was quite hesitant to let us do so.

We soon found out why. He was waiting for someone. It was a couple of someone's, and they looked to be high on something. One of them was massive in stature, not unlike my friend. One of them went directly up to the young man, shaking him violently with his clothes in his fists. He yelled to the man, "Please, Chris, stop! I don't have anything!" It was obvious then, this had to do with drugs, and we were witnessing something we shouldn't be. But their actions were not going to slip by me, so I told them simply to go...leave the kid alone. Since he didn't respond or let the kid go, I grabbed him by the back of his collar to pull him off. He went right back to the kid to grab him. Once again...I tugged him away, even throwing him to the ground and reiterating that he needed to just leave.

So far, the bigger half of the goon squad was doing nothing, and my own massive bodybuilder friend Rod was literally sitting on a nearby wall, head bowed in prayer. I would have liked more active and present help from my friend than that. Out of the blue, the two punks started walking away, and I could now see that the bigger man had a baseball bat. Well, something inside me snapped and I followed them. I yelled, "Jesus loves you!" They kept walking, but the bigger man said to back off. I yelled again, "NO! Jesus loves you!" Well, I guess the big guy had heard enough because he yelled back, "I will give you Jesus," and began running full bore at me with the bat.

I stood completely still but bowed my head and silently asked for help. I knew he was about ten yards from me and closing the distance very quickly. My eyes were still closed in prayer when I heard two shrill shrieks. I opened my eyes to see the two men scrambling to get back onto their feet over the top of each other and trying to get away as fast as they could. They had ended up about thirty yards from me in the span of two seconds. It was like they were thrown by something. Was it just the being thrown that made them shriek? Did they see something? To this day this event absolutely astounds me, and I cannot explain it in rational terms. Whatever happened was so strange and powerful that it terrified me. I never ministered on the streets again, and my friend Rod missed the entire thing, as he had his head down the whole time.

Time passed and I ended up being a church pastor for children. There were several families that all lived on the same street, and they all took vacations within a couple of months of each other. Three families over this time period asked me, my wife Sharon, and our children to house-sit. We were in each home from a week to three weeks at a time.

One home felt very off, stale almost. One night we had gone to sleep and I awoke to the feeling of being strangled, and Sharon was wheezing. I could also hear the kids crying in the other room. I choked out the words, "Get off me." It released me and I immediately begin praying for Sharon and left the room to check on the kids. They only said they had a horrible dream. I reassured them and encouraged them to try to go back to sleep. Upon returning to the master bedroom, something caught my eye in the corner. A massive, murky gray tentacle was reversing back up into the air vent. It was at least eight feet long and had initially been hanging all the way to the floor. Sharon was frozen in place, staring at this thing. My anger rose quickly, and I began shouting at it to leave. And even though it was out of sight, I was going room to room, continuing to shout...because I could sense where it was. I pursued it until I felt it leave. It never came back, and the house felt completely different. It was peaceful in the home during the rest of our stay.

Later, we were over with this very family for dinner when something extremely trivial happened...like the spill of a glass of water. The father proceeded to absolutely snap and went into a rage over it. It seemed so unnatural, because this man wasn't a drinker, no drugs, and the family seemed very nice and straitlaced. I will not say much more about it, only that I knew there were some dark things going on in their home.

The last occurrence I will share happened back in the '90s, and it was after my time as a minister. I decided to try to make it as a full-time musician, and some friends of mine were interested in working on a joint project. The idea was to do both original works and covers. We had the whole setup in the garage—drums, amps, guitars, you name it.

One of the covers we kept practicing over and over and had down pretty damn well was 'Don't Fear the Reaper' by The Blue Oyster Cult. During one session we got to the actual portion of the song where you utilize the words *don't fear the reaper*—it was maybe the third chorus in—when another voice came through the PA. It wasn't human at all, deep and guttural...and it came from all around us. It was much louder than us, well above the sounds of singing through our mics and amp. Truth be told, it was off-key to boot. We all heard it, stopped playing, and my friends immediately began packing up to leave. We were all honestly pretty freaked out. My take on it was...man, we really tapped into the essence of that song!

As a side note...we always recorded our sessions so we could improve upon things we heard and didn't like. I instantly went to the tape and played it...the deep voice was there, singing away. I even played it for my wife, who was stunned. The next day, I went to play it again...it was completely gone. Only our voices and instruments remained embedded within. I found out later from a neighbor that the man who lived in our home prior had killed himself after losing his family and being unable to break out of a deep state of depression. After hearing that voice come through, our project hit a wall, and they never came back to my home to play. Turns out in this case…there was reason to fear the reaper.

FRANKLIN AND THE TROLL

*W*hat *if your parents assume your imaginary friend is nothing more than that, but there is soon proof to the contrary? An entity named Franklin had no problem letting his living roommates know he was very real. As if that wasn't enough, Wil was told by Franklin that his brother John also inhabited the home and 'wasn't nice'. The area John most liked to make his presence known—why, the basement, of course.*

***

I was six when my family moved to a small

town in Minnesota and into a house that would leave me with so many memories. It was a beautiful and roomy property in town, with lovely country touches. Very shortly after moving in, I began to tell my mom and dad about my good friend Franklin. He was my constant, welcome companion. Problem was, I guess, that Franklin wasn't real. Not real to anyone but me, that is. My parents just wrote it off as something normal kids go through. Oh, Wil's got an imaginary friend...how cute!

I believe my father was the first to realize there was something strange going on. One night, he came upstairs to tell me to go to bed, only to find me fast asleep. That was all well and good until he could clearly see in from the doorway...some of my toys moving by themselves. He only admitted to witnessing this event years later, and he still slightly scoffs at the paranormal. Franklin never scared me or made me feel uncomfortable, but this wasn't something my entire family would agree on.

Franklin made it a point to tell me that his brother John lived in the basement...and that he wasn't a nice fellow. I told my parents this, which of course made them wonder...but not really worry. Not at first, anyway. My mother was home alone one day, and the sound of voices and very loud banging started coming from the basement. Now, this was one of the old farmhouse types where the basement door was in the kitchen. You could lie on the floor and see through the stairs to the basement space underneath. The very first time she heard the sounds, she lay down to take a look, only to see a massive cooler slide across the floor below. She jumped up, locked the door...and called my dad to tell him to come home from work, immediately. He was a long way off, so he had a friend of his come check the house while my mom waited outside. There was no one to be found. She heard the sounds again after that, but just did her best to ignore them.

As it turns out, John and Franklin were, in

fact, very real people and owned the home back in the 1930s. When it comes to the property itself, a couple of things stand out and make it possible to form a snapshot of the brothers' lives out on the farm. There are a couple of things to glean from some items left on the property and from the structure itself. The first, an easy and assumptive guess about it being a working farm at one point, because I would often tell my parents things about farming that a six-year-old shouldn't have known. Franklin obviously enjoyed talking about his work. Second, there was not only a tunnel that led into the basement area, but rows of shelving lined with jars full of screws and various implements that you might use to work on cars. My dad always thought this area doubled as a repair shop, which could make John a mechanic in his day. It's only a guess, but it might make sense as to why John was attached to that area of the home over others, after spending many an hour down in the basement, honing his craft and making a living.

My mom tells a story of going to a parent-teacher conference, and the teacher asked her how the farm was. My mom was obviously slightly confused by this. The teacher proceeded to tell her that I would constantly talk of milking cows, doing chores, and other everyday farm-life activities. My knowledge of farming far exceeded the norm for a young man who had never lived on a functioning farm.

As far as what Franklin looked like, I honestly don't remember. I just know he was friendly enough to me, and it was certainly astonishing to find out that he was not imaginary at all.

The next phenomenon I will tell you about occurred when I was fourteen, and it was during the summertime. I know this for a fact because it was a weekday and I was wide awake at 1 a.m., just hanging in the living room, watching some TV in the dark on low volume, because my dad was upstairs sleeping. We had a couch against the left-hand side of the room, and I was situated with my back against the armrest. In my peripheral vision, I saw something moving across the room.

I turned my head completely towards it and saw nothing. I went back to watching TV, thinking nothing of it. Until...there was movement yet again. I turned my head a little quicker this time, and again, all I could make out was the normal shadows of the furniture that the glow of the TV was casting. I honestly just thought it was the dog, but I then spotted him on the other side of the room, fast asleep. So, back to the TV again. A few minutes later, more movement. This time I decided not to turn towards it, but slowly positioned my body so that I would be able to see the area easier. As I carefully repositioned myself, I could still see the movement. My heart raced, and the questions of what it could be kept filling my mind. When I finally completed the transition, what my eyes saw was unimaginable and surreal.

Standing there, lit by the glow of the TV, was a creature about three feet tall with blue-gray skin and long black greasy hair. With intense eyes, it stared at me. A variety of thoughts were running simultaneously through my mind, like *What the hell is that? Why hasn't the dog woken up? Where did it come from?* and *What do I do now?* But just as my mind was coming to grips with what was there in plain sight in front of me, it was gone. Just like that, it vanished, and all in the blink of my eye. I immediately jumped up to turn on every light downstairs and began to look for it. I tore through the house, looking behind furniture, in closets, everywhere, but it was gone. Just like that, it was there; then it was gone, leaving no trace behind, nothing that I could use to say it was real or show anyone to prove I'd seen what I know I saw.

That night was a sleepless one. I lay contemplating what it was I had seen. I searched my thoughts for a simple answer but found none. Even after all these years I am still bothered by the sight of that grotesque-looking creature. When I try now to identify what it could have been, the only thing that comes to mind is a troll. But how is that possible? I know what I saw though, and I didn't make it up or dream it.

So, there you go, trolls, if that's what it was, do exist. They are not just relegated to children's fables and horror movies; they also appear to young kids, leaving their lives filled with nightmares. But maybe that's what it was there to do all along.

INCUBUS

*A*nn has experienced poltergeist-like disturbances in her home since the age of four. One might quickly label it as such, but what happens as she ages gives her pause on its true form. Whatever this thing is, it is very dark and demented and is powerful enough to interact physically with her. This is ongoing activity of the worst kind. Extremely invasive and personal, and it seems to get pure joy from making her feel exhausted and highly vulnerable.

***

When I was four years old, we lived in a very old farmhouse. The heating system was so old that on some very cold winter nights we would all sleep in the living room. I remember once sleeping next to my dad by the fireplace and waking up to see some of the firewood moving by itself. I was, of course, a very young girl at the time and didn't understand what exactly that could mean, so I just snuggled back up with my dad and fell asleep. Many times, there was a little girl who would want to play with me. I would be sleeping and end up in the room she wanted me to play in, which would get me in a good deal of trouble with my mom. I had a hard time discerning if that was real or not.

Once my siblings and I were adults, we all started sharing our various experiences in that home. One recurring encounter we all shared was a mother-type figure entity that would walk to each of our rooms and stand in our doorways. We would even call out to one another, "She's heading to your room now!" It became normal to us, just part of a routine. Even my mother ended up admitting seeing this figure sometimes, but my dad never did.

He didn't believe any of it was going on, and even later when he did see some odd things...he would never admit to it happening. My sister was sick at one point, and the figure walked over to her bed and sat on the edge in an attempt to comfort her. What's interesting is, my dad remodeled the house, and you could see her walking through the hallway and into a closet that used to be another hallway. Sometimes she would even sit in a rocking chair that sat in the corner of my brother's room, which scared him greatly...he would put his blanket over his head in an attempt to sleep.

On another occasion, my mom and dad had gotten in a fight, and we happened to have the extended family over for dinner. While everyone was sitting at the table in the dining room, several dishes in the kitchen came off the stove and smashed on the floor. It was a good distance from where they had been sitting on the stove to where they hit on the floor. Something had to have essentially carried them or thrown them with great force to that spot. All fourteen people over for dinner saw it, even my dad...but he found a way to dismiss it. It seemed to feed off the energy of our house.

When I was in high school, I started having something interact with me when I was sleeping. It would start at my feet, touching lightly...moving up to my knees, up to my hips, and get to the point where it would pull the covers completely off me, and that's when I thought, ok...I'll just get up, then. I had no clue what was going on, and it certainly frightened me.

Once I had my children, the activity around me ramped up significantly. I was awake in the middle of the night, tending to my infant child, and decided to open the curtains and look outside. I can't even tell you why I did it. There was a light across the street that caught my eye...it was not a perfect circle, but misshaped. I couldn't figure out what it was, so I closed the curtains and got my baby calmed and situated. I went back to bed, only to soon feel something lie on top of me. It was extremely heavy. Its weight settled on me as one would lie down...foot to head. As it got to the pillow, I could hear it brush against my ear. It got worse. A few nights later, I put the kids to bed, and it happened again. It lay directly on top of me, and I was completely unable to move or make a sound. All I will say is, this time...it was very inappropriate with me, and it went on long enough for it to do what it wanted with me. I cannot tell you how upsetting this event was. And it certainly seemed to make clear...it could do what it wanted, when it wanted.

Moving houses did nothing to keep it away; it always followed. I had just moved into an apartment and was taking a shower. I felt a painful burning sensation on the back of my leg, near the top of my calf, and it was bruised. From the shape and size, it looked to me like a bite. I had my pastor come over to look, and he confirmed my initial assessment of it. It also looked like a bite to him. I certainly could not have reached there myself to inflict this mark. I was also having horrible dreams where it was at the end of my bed and it was trying to get to me, so even when it 'wasn't really' there, it was tormenting me.

A couple of years later I moved into the home I'm in now and stayed a couple of nights alone (no internet hooked up...you know how kids are). On the very first night, something came running into my room and it hit the side of my wooden bed...knocking on it repeatedly. It then proceeded to get up on the bed and straddle me at waist level. This was a terrible realization that certainly no matter where I went, it would follow. Three months later I was getting ready for work, standing in the bathroom drying my hair, when I saw a distinct bite mark on my tricep. It was painful to the touch. Again, there was no way I could have reached this part of my body and do this to myself.

One night after work, I came home and fell

asleep on the couch, and I heard it walk through my kitchen and into the living room. It put its hand underneath my head and lifted my head up and dropped it heavily back onto the couch. This was a benign incident to be honest, because this being is quite powerful and has no problem moving me where it wants, and on several occasions has flipped me completely over from my back to my stomach. As if this isn't strange and terrifying enough...it once got in bed with me and made its way up to my pillow. This time, I could not feel the weight or presence of it anywhere but my pillow. And this will sound very strange, but I could hear and feel its 'wings' on my face and my ear.

I have unfortunately caught glimpses of it, and it does have black feathers covering some parts of it. Size-wise I always assumed it was the size of a normal human being, but when that event happened, I could not figure out how it was small enough to crouch on the pillow next to me.

It will come to me nightly for weeks at a time and wear me down to where I'm completely exhausted. And just when I think it may be gone for good, it starts up again. When it comes around, it is extremely hard to get up in the morning, and I feel like I have a weight on my back all day. It's as if it wants me in a vulnerable state as much as possible, and there doesn't seem to be any pattern to it. The only thing I've ever noticed sometimes being the same is it will often wake me up at 3:18 a.m. I've even woken to it saying my name, and it can sound like my mother, a friend, or even just a random voice of a stranger. I know this all may sound pretty crazy, and how could anyone live in a situation like this...but all I can say is, when it almost becomes a norm, and this is the hand you're dealt in life...you just have to find a way to deal with it. It's pretty amazing what a person can get used to. This is, of course, not to say I ever enjoyed it or didn't want it to leave.

I did seek help at various points. A friend

of mine mentioned that his mom was a psychic and could do a reading on me. He went inside to start introductions, leaving me outside. She wouldn't even come to the door or let me in. She insisted I leave immediately because she could see a black mass attached to my shoulders. She was near hysterics explaining this.

I also at one point went to a counselor who had known me and my family for some time. I did not tell her at first what was going on with me, but slowly started mentioning the events. She mentioned something interesting to me...that maybe I had something in my possession that the entity was attached to. Around that time, my grandfather, my father, and my uncles were Masons. I mentioned to her that my mother had given me my grandmother's Eastern Star. Her immediate reaction was, "You need to get that out of your house."

A little background on my family as it pertains to Masons...my father's entire family were/are Masons. So his great-great-grandfather was a Mason...and so on, and so on. So, this equates to all my grandmothers having been married to Masons. The meetings were always private and included the men only. A story my mother told me (my dad never shared anything about the Masonic religion) was that my great-grandmother and some of the other wives were curious about what really went on in these secret meetings. Keep in mind, this was the period when women wore bonnets. The women snuck over to the meeting and watched silently from the brush. Music began to emit from an initially unseen source...but soon they saw it. It was a banjo moving around the group and playing of its own accord. It scared the women so badly that they ran back across the field as fast as they could. While they ran, something kept untying their bonnets at their chins again and again. Some might speculate that what the wives had done that night caught the ire of something dark. Something that follows me to this day.

I am not the only one of my siblings who has odd things happening to them as an adult. My sister can shake someone's hand and from that contact alone...tell if they're a good person or not. My brother told me that during his line of work in commercial refrigeration (this specific job was at a bar), he and his co-worker were talking with the new owner. After the owner walked away, he told his co-worker, "This guy's not going to be here next year." The co-worker was obviously confused, but my brother insisted on the fact that the man didn't have much longer. Less than a year later, they went back to do more work, and the man had indeed passed. Another story that includes my brother...I was preschool age (all my siblings were at least ten years older than me) and I told my mother out of the blue, "I miss Bobby." She gave me a very confused look, so I repeated it again. Bobby was my brother's best friend, and he was murdered at a convenience store shortly after.

The last part of this I will tell you unfortunately includes my son. I was divorced from his dad, and he was living with me. The first time he experienced anything, he was fourteen years old, and it caused an extreme anxiety attack. It was the middle of the night, and he didn't want to explain it much...but he just said, "Something's messing with me." My heart sank immediately. He was not aware of what I was going through. The last thing you want to do is frighten your children, and I thought maybe the divorce had triggered some intense stress in him. But the activity continued around him as well. He complained that something would scream in his ear, and it wasn't human. And that he's even had the same sensation I have...of something lying on top of him and rendering him unable to move. This entity has also touched him inappropriately. There was now no denying what the cause was. I still tried to keep quiet about it, trying to figure out what to do...how to help him. That night, I had a horrible night's sleep, riddled with terrible dreams, and found out he did too. Turns out, we had a shared dream experience where we were both frantically trying to get to each other but couldn't. He's seen very little of it with his own eyes, but he knows it's a male entity. Even my daughter who stays with me on weekends is beginning to have dreams that I would identify as being about or from the same entity.

The level of helplessness that I feel in this situation is staggering. Up to this point, I've talked to pastors, counselors, and even had the house blessed. Nothing seems to help for long. I don't know what will become of me, but I can tell you that I'm living in hell. I pray daily that one day this will all come to an end so I can live my life.

UPDATE SINCE ORIGINAL AIR DATE ON 11/29/2019

I put Ann in touch with Jon-Paul Capece, MTS.

He has been on my show several times to talk demonology and is well-versed in these subjects and types of cases. I am incredibly happy to report that after months of contact with Ann, and upon following Jon-Paul's advice, things have, according to Ann, "Been quiet so far." I hope this reprieve continues and I wish Ann and her family well. A huge thanks to my good friend Jon-Paul for his help in this case.

GRAVEYARD TERROR

*E*VP, *or electronic voice phenomena, are sounds found on electronic recordings. Every ghost hunter and enthusiast takes recording devices with them on investigations with hopes of capturing a ghostly voice. What happens though when the voice manifests itself in different ways? Well, for two sixteen-year-old amateur ghost hunters, they found out that the voices on the recorder can do just that.*

***

I was sixteen at the time and it was the mid-1980s. Long before the renaissance and popularity of ghost-hunting shows, I thought I was on my way to possibly becoming a paranormal ghost hunter like Hans Holzer. I had the heard ghosts on tape courtesy of my older brother, who happened to work for a state park where a proper and professional paranormal investigation had taken place. He showed up at the house one day, excited to share with me his treasure. He knew I had an interest in such things, as he did too. He sat me down and pressed the play button. I intently listened as the investigator talked; then I heard it. The voice sounded odd like it came from somewhere else. It's hard to explain, but it was there. My brother hit stop, rewound the tape, and played it again. Upon hearing it again, my eyes widened with joy, fascination, and a bit of fear. I'll admit, while I'm very curious and intrigued about such things, I do get scared; well, maybe that's part of the fun, you know, the exhilaration or thrill.

There was no mistaking the voices and what they were saying. My middle brother thought they were fake, which of course resulted in an argument and debate erupting.

Nope, I was convinced, and there was nothing that was going to stop me from getting my own ghosts on tape.

I immediately purchased a microcassette recorder, recruited my good friend Dave, and planned just how we'd capture the sounds and voices of ghosts on tape. Dave was all in. Like me, he loved all things horror and paranormal and couldn't wait to see what we could get.

Our plan was to go to a graveyard in the middle of the night. Our rationale was based upon the fact or assumption that ghosts are there because...well, it's a graveyard, and two, doing it at night would add a layer of fright for us. We were fortunate, as we lived in Southern Maryland and happened to be surrounded by dozens of graveyards, many with old sections, some dating back to the 1700s. With our plan set, and the specific graveyard chosen, we went out on a cold and moonless night in early December to record some ghosts.

As we exited my Jeep and slowly marched towards the graveyard, I pulled out my microcassette player and readied it. I still recall we were more excited than scared. As soon as my foot touched the edge of the graveyard, I pressed the play/record button. The recorder came to life, a small red light appeared, and the reels squeaked as the tape coursed through the player, going from one side of the cassette to the next.

We slowly meandered through the vast graveyard, stopping at headstones that looked interesting. At each stop, we'd recite the epitaph etched in the granite, hoping that our brief interaction would incite a ghost to speak. We proceeded from one to the next until the recorder stopped, giving us an hour of recording to listen to. We both decided that it was best not to stay there and listen, so we packed up and headed to my house.

Upon arriving at my house and warming up with a hot chocolate, we pressed the play button and settled in with our hopes high.

Well, it took all of fifteen seconds to get our first EVP. It had happened the second we stepped foot in the graveyard.

Dave had said, "Let's take a look at some of these graves." What followed sent chills down my spine.

There's no mistaking the voice and what it says, and I'll say now that it didn't sound as if it came from our dimension. I know that sounds weird, but it doesn't sound like it came from something earthly. The second Dave finished what he was saying, a deep and sinister voice snapped, "GO AWAY!" I know if we had heard that there, we would have turned around instantly and ran off.

Thrilled that we had gotten a voice so quickly, we proceeded to carefully listen to the tape, taking notes at each point we felt we heard something. When we were done, we had discovered three other instances, from something clearly reciting the Lord's Prayer to whispers that were hard to make out. We were beyond impressed with ourselves and were now determined to go back out again the next night.

Saturday night came and we were back out there, same graveyard, same time, but we took a different route, and this time Dave had a recorder. Our plan was to split up and get twice as many.

We recorded an hour's worth and promptly headed back to my house. Again, we discovered voices on both of our recorders, with some overlapping. One would be louder on mine while on his it seemed more distant; this gave us the clue that there is a proximity to the voices or the spirits. The most disturbing sound we got came from a grave with the name Rebecca S. Brooks. She had died in the late 1700s at the age of forty-nine, and with no mention of a spouse or children, we assumed she was single, something not typical for back then. What I recorded on there was unlike anything we'd gotten before. As I was reciting her name, I began to stutter, something I don't do. Not a second after I spoke her name, a loud growl or bark is heard on the recording. It's as loud as my voice, and when the speed of the tape is slowed, it's a distinct guttural growl.

Dave, who was about twenty feet away, also got it, but it was faint.

I was not a fan of the growl. I thought it meant we'd come upon something dark or evil. An entity that was not just an angry spirit but something more. The growl left us a bit freaked, but we were more determined than ever to get more recordings.

A week passed and we set out again. This time we'd go in the daytime to the same graveyard. Like the last session, we each had a recorder, split up, and paced a different part of the cemetery. Like the other times, we got voices, and the most memorable from that day came from a gravesite of a family that had died on the same day in the 1940s. On my recorder I heard children laughing. It's clear as day, and you can tell one was a boy and one was a girl.

Dave, who was feet away, also recorded the children, and like before, the voices seemed more distant, meaning I was next to them.

We couldn't get enough of what we were doing. In fact, I think we were getting obsessed. All I could do at night during the week was think about getting back out there, and I couldn't get past Rebecca S. Brooks. I kept trying to imagine what she looked like, why was she single, and why did something, if not her, growl at me in anger at her gravesite? Dave and I began to wonder if she was a witch. I know that sounds cliché, but that's what our theory was at the time.

During all this time my mother was getting concerned. She wasn't a fan of the paranormal and with my fascination with the occult and all things mysterious. While she didn't sanction my nightly graveyard visits to record, she didn't forbid me from doing it either.

Another weekend came and Dave and I went to the initial Maryland settlement site, which was founded in 1634. It was a day trip and we recorded a few things. We just couldn't believe our luck. It seemed everywhere we went, we got something very distinct and clear on the tape. This wasn't like the shows where you have to 'think' you heard something. On the tapes we made, you could clearly hear the voice and what they said. I recall on our trip to St. Mary's City, we got a response to a question posed. We found an old grave dated to the late 1600s. A massive oak tree was now growing out of the center of it, the trunk so big that the headstone was displaced at a forty-degree angle. We asked if there was a spirit there and if they were upset about the tree. On the tape we got a series of wood-knocking sounds. Question asked and answered. We couldn't be more convinced and happier.

Our ability to score voices using simple microcassette players made us think that if we had more sophisticated devices and equipment, we could become legit ghost hunters. We began to do research on getting the gear, not an easy thing to do in the mid-1980s.

With our heads full of ourselves almost to the point of chest thumping, we set out on another late-night graveyard session. The site, an old abandoned cemetery overgrown with vines and trees. If someone was looking for a set to film a horror movie, this was it.

We pulled the Jeep down a narrow dirt drive and parked in one of the few clear spaces. We jumped out, recorders and flashlights in hand, although that night we did have a half moon to provide some light. It was frigid, but I was warm with excitement about what cool things we'd record.

We waded through the tall dry grasses until we reached the edge; we pushed through a rusted metal gate and entered. Large trees and vines had taken over the cemetery. What headstones we could see appeared incredibly old and showed the signs of many years of weathering and neglect.

Not skipping a beat, we both hit record and went to work. I went left and Dave pushed straight ahead. I came upon a headstone, the etched name and dates almost impossible to read, but I gave it my best. Not twenty feet from me I could hear Dave reading a headstone, the beam of his flashlight zeroed in on the words.

I chuckled at how much fun this was. We were constantly hitting pay dirt, and when we could afford it, we'd have even better gear. I proceeded to the next headstone. It was tall, standing just shy of four feet, and the granite was weathered heavily. I cast my flashlight on it and saw the name Elizabeth Thompson; below were simply the birthdate and death dates, nothing else. Like Rebecca's headstone, I noticed that Elizabeth too had died in her forties and with nothing else mentioned like 'wife of so and so'. I had to assume she was single and unmarried like Rebecca had been. I read her name and cited her birth and death dates, then moved on, not thinking anything of it.

The hour went by quickly and we headed back to the Jeep. Both of us were dripping with excitement. We just knew we had recorded something. Heck, we were batting a thousand, and we had zero doubt this graveyard wouldn't let us down. It looked haunted, so therefore it had to be, our young minds thought.

I went to start the Jeep when Dave suggested we listen to the recordings there.

I hesitated and questioned if we should.

Without too many words, he gave an adequate explanation and had me convinced.

We both settled back and played mine first. As we listened, we struggled but didn't hear anything. Of course, we weren't too disappointed, as there were still a solid forty-some odd minutes left on the tape, and the odds were in our favor.

The tape got to the point where I was at Elizabeth Thompson's headstone. We heard my voice clear as day then promptly following were three loud and angry growls.

I stopped the tape and shot Dave a wide-eyed look. I could see the fear in his eyes too, but something told me to listen again. I rewound the tape and played it again.

The growls were exactly like the one we had recorded at Rebecca's grave. It was then that a heavy feeling washed over me and Dave.

"Let's get out of here," he said.

"Yeah, let's do that," I replied and tossed the recorder into the backseat.

The heavy feeling became crushing, my senses were tingling, and I just knew that something else was there with us. I'm getting goosebumps just writing this story and recalling it.

I turned the key in the ignition and tapped the gas pedal, but nothing happened. This couldn't be happening, I thought, my Jeep was only a couple of years old and barely had any miles on it, yet here it was having an electrical problem.

Dave screamed, "Start it up!"

"I'm trying," I barked back, fear in my voice.

The heavy presence grew.

Feverishly I tried several more times, but all the engine did was click and the headlights flickered. "Start up!" I hollered, my voice cracking with fear.

"Hurry up, start the Jeep!" Dave again cried out.

"I'm trying," I barked back as I tried two more times but still the same results. Not knowing what else to do, I paused, pressed my eyes closed, and said a quick prayer to God. I turned the key again and the engine roared to life. I slammed the Jeep into gear and sped off.

Dave and I sat in silence the entire ride home. After arriving, we both agreed not to listen to the tape again until another time.

That night as I lay in bed, I stared out the window, fully expecting to see whatever it was hovering outside.

Dave and I never went out again. That one terrifying night put the nail in our coffin so to speak. Something was in the Jeep with us, and it wasn't happy that we had come to the old St. Andrews cemetery. I don't know if it felt disrespected by our presence or was just evil; heck, maybe it was simply messing with us. All I know is both Dave and I felt whatever was there, it didn't feel nice, and it had a real effect on the electrical system in my Jeep.

There is always much debate over ghosts and the paranormal. For me, I'm a true believer, and nothing anyone can say would move or change my opinion. To this day I still have those tapes but don't have a player to listen to them. Maybe I shouldn't mess with it, as I'd hate to have whatever that was show up again.

WENDIGO IN IOWA

*T*here are some encounters shared with me that I don't have to ponder long if I'd ever want to experience it myself. It would be a hard pass. Staunchly on my 'No List'. This episode was one of those. A road sighting when it comes to, say, a Bigfoot is often mentioned as an ideal situation. You're relatively safe in something mobile...you identify something highly peculiar, and then away you're whisked. But in this case, what is seen on an early morning drive to work not once, but twice...had the witness so shaken, she almost ran off the road. The emaciated and terrifying creature on that lonely, dark stretch of road was just the beginning of her and her family's nightmare.

***

What you're about to read was something I'd kept to myself since it happened in August of 2017, not even telling my husband until I had told Shannon about it on her show.

My encounter happened in rural Iowa just outside the small town where I still live. With limited opportunities for work where I live, I found a job in a much larger city, which meant I had to commute. On a good day, my drive one way was an hour and a half. This job required me to be at work by five in the morning, so this put me on long stretches of highway in the very early hours.

What I disliked most, besides having to make the long drive, was having to do it at such an hour, and during this time I was pregnant. Just being on those dark and lonely roads was something I'm not a fan of.

The early morning in question it appeared to be darker than usual, but I'm sure some of that is my memory. Either way, it was a dark and clear night, not a cloud in the sky, and the stars were bright.

I had only been on the road for about ten minutes when my headlights touched on something on the left-hand side of the road, on the shoulder, just past a small bridge, which spanned a creek below. Being that this is rural Iowa, I imagined it was an animal, so I started to slow down just in case it decided to jump out in front of me. I closed the gap on whatever it was, but unlike an animal, it didn't move. I didn't think much of it at the time and thought it could be a piece of equipment, as it was pretty big.

I drew closer, close enough to now see it wasn't a piece of equipment and that it appeared to be a human. Its torso was long, and it just sat on the shoulder facing the road. I leaned closer to the steering wheel to get a better look and noticed its knees were pulled up tight to its chest with its long thin arms wrapped around them. I made out its hands and slender fingers, which grasped its knobby knees. It had its gazed fixed in the direction I was going and not at me...yet.

I was alarmed but now just thought it was a person, not some sort of monster. I did find it odd that someone would be out sitting on the side of the road at three thirty in the morning.

I got a bit closer when it hit me that this wasn't a person; it was just too big and tall to be a human. If I had to guess, I'd say it was probably eight feet tall if it stood. I could make this estimate based upon how long its torso was as well as how long its legs were. It was thin, as if it were emaciated, and I saw no clothing. The skin on its body was black, or a dark gray and covered in dark hair. I remember because of how my headlights made it shine as if it was wet, like it had just crawled out of the creek below. The one thing that struck me was that while the skin on the body was dark, its face was white, like bone white. I couldn't get a good look at its eyes because the hair on its head hung down over its forehead and covered some of its face. Looking back now, I'm glad I couldn't see its eyes; something about looking into the gaze of something like that would have made it worse.

All I could think now was that this was wrong. This wasn't a person, there was no way. That then begged the question, if this wasn't a person, what was it?

I had slowed well below the posted speed limit but was still headed towards it, with fear rising each foot closer I got. Just as I was about to pass it, the thing turned its head and stared at me.

A stab of panic spread across my body as I stared back at this thing. I pressed down hard on the accelerator and checked to make sure my doors were locked. I looked in my rearview mirror and side mirrors to ensure it wasn't coming after me as I sped off.

It took me a while to calm down. I couldn't shake it though as I questioned what I'd seen and wondered if I had hallucinated it. About halfway into my drive, I came up on the next town and found a place to stop. After getting some water and a much-needed break, I was back on the road.

I wasn't on the road more than ten minutes when I spotted the creature again just when I crested the top of a steep hill. This time now it was crouched in the middle of the road like it was waiting for me. Its body positioning gave me the impression it was about to spring or leap.

I screamed, and with a white-knuckle grip on the steering wheel, I swerved around it. I slammed my foot on the pedal and raced away, not letting up until I reached my work.

Having sped, I got to work early, and I was grateful for that. I took the time to sit in my car in the parking lot and get a hold of myself.

I feel my co-workers sensed something was off that day, as I was quieter than normal, but never said a word about what I'd seen.

Not long after, I had a medical emergency, went to the emergency room, and almost had a miscarriage. Thankfully, I didn't lose my baby, but I question if this thing could have had an effect or my medical issue was simply a result of stress, as my doctor suspected. My job was stressful already, then I saw that thing, and those two things combined could have resulted in so much stress that I almost lost my baby.

After leaving the hospital, I did quit my job.

Much time went by and I was listening to another podcast. They mentioned a creature called a wendigo, I immediately looked it up, and the images that popped up reminded me so much of what I'd seen that I froze in fear as I looked at them. It was right after that that I decided to share my story and contacted Shannon.

Wanting to be armed with information, I researched wendigos and discovered two theories about possibly why I encountered the creature.

First, numerous Native American tribes detail wendigo as harbingers or messengers that something bad is about to occur. This made me wonder if it could have been there to be a warning about the medical emergency and that my long drives and stressful job weren't good for my health and that of my baby.

Or, the second theory, which is more sinister. That it was there to be the cause of my medical emergency. That it wanted to harm me and my child. That is frightening to even ponder. Something so evil wanted to harm me and wanted to kill my child.

I'll never really know what I saw, but the effects are still with me. Even though I have some peace of mind after sharing, I still worry anytime I'm on those roads in the late or early morning hours.

IN CONCLUSION

The life-changing aspects of these encounters can get lost in the details of what a creature, entity, or whatever it was experienced looked like, how it moved, etc. The other fascinating and, to me, even more important element is what it did to the person. Much like those in our first book on Bigfoot, some choose never to go in the woods again. And that is a much easier fix than what you have just encountered within these pages. Many could not just pick up and move when faced with something terrifying or invasive, and occasionally, even when they did, they were simply followed by it.

One of the ultimate 'be careful what you wish for' situations occurs when an active and involved 'ghost hunter' inadvertently brings something home. They go out in search of that spooky experience, have it...but also carry the assumption of being able to leave it behind. It seems to be a rare occurrence, but is it even what we think of as a ghost? That classic, earthbound spirit of a person who just can't seem to cross over? Or is it something else entirely? Something darker or ingrained with a trickster side to it. A demonic entity (these seem to get fingers pointed at them far too often), a fae, or elemental, or even simply a light anomaly manifesting itself. The shock of an encounter with any of these listed above is often, not surprisingly, so jarring, few speak of them even to family members and close friends.

With my own experience of seeing the shadow beings in the woods that day, I tend to lean towards the theory that any, if not all, of these things are in essence running tandem to us at any given moment during our time on this plane of existence. Some people have one-off meetings, while others are plagued (others call it gifted) with paranormal occurrences. I suppose you have to ask yourself if you'd rather stay a bystander or choose to seek out that ultimate confirmation experience that ends up keeping you tucked in extra tight under the covers each night.

I'll wrap this all up by saying that no matter if you're the person who finds the experience a gift or a curse, what's happened is you've had a step or glimpse into a much larger world.

I want to thank each and every one who contributed to this book, especially those who shared their stories, and I'd like to express gratitude to my listeners. You have listened to my podcast, *iNTO THE FRAY*, and now for a second time have journeyed with me beyond. Look for more to come...

ABOUT THE AUTHORS

Shannon LeGro has been examining the paranormal since she was a teen after having her own personal experience She strives to bring a fresh perspective and an open mind to the most intriguing mysteries in our universe. She is the host & producer of the popular podcast, iNTO THE FRAY and can also be heard as a guest host on the show Midnight In Desert. You can also see her in the Small Town Monsters production, On the Trail of Bigfoot and in the upcoming documentary, On the Trail of UFOs.

Visit Shannon online at www.intothefrayradio.com

G. Michael Hopf is the USA Today bestselling author of almost forty novels including his international bestselling post-apocalyptic series, THE NEW WORLD. He has made a prominent name for himself in both the post-apocalyptic and western genres. He is co-founder of Beyond The Fray Publishing & Doomsday Press. He is a combat veteran of the United States Marine Corps and whiskey aficionado.

Visit G. Michael Hopf at www.gmichaelhopf.com

Made in the USA
Monee, IL
13 July 2020